DEVELOPMENT AND SOCIAL JUSTICE

DEVELOPMENT AND SOCIAL JUSTICE
A Legal Perspective

Dr. Priya Rao

KALPAZ

Development and Social Justice : A Legal Perspective

ISBN: 978-81-7835-927-4

Published in 2012 in India by
Kalpaz Publications
C-30, Satyawati Nagar,
Delhi-110052
E-mail: kalpaz@hotmail.com
Phone : 9212729499

Lasser Type Setting : Quick Media, Delhi
Printed at : Chawla Offset Printers, Delhi

Contents

Foreword

"Development and Social Justice : A Legal Perspective" is a collection of articles written by Dr. Priya Rao during the recent past relating to development and Social Justice. The subject varies from general theme of common man's access to justice Delivery system to more specific themes such as, rights of children and women, right to information, policy of affirmative action, criterion for social and economic backwardness, issue of other backward classes and higher education etc. There are more than one article on the theme of women empowerment, education, affirmative action and protective discrimination, and other backward classes. Other themes which appeared in selective manner relate to enforcement of Disasters management Laws and Politics of Global Warming.

Although the papers vary in themes, there is a common thread that runs through most of the papers. It is the concern about the interface of development with social justice. The main concern that the author expresses is about the tendency of the development to bypass the excluded and marginalised groups from the benefits of the development. The growth tends to be non-exclusive in character particularly for the marginalised groups. The author discussed the problem of children, women and other backward classes. The author argued that despite growth these groups remain neglected and pointed out the limits of the development. Given this limitation of the particular type of development model, the author argued for special policies in the form of affirmative action and protective discrimination for children, women, and backward classes. The legal dimensions of the affirmative action policies has been discussed in a very clear manner. The author particularly discuss the contradiction between the customary law and practices and the secular law. This law in fact posed the main challenge for realisation of rights by the citizens due to the contradictions.

The another theme that is addressed is the resilience of Tradition towards Modernity. It is necessary that tradition must give way to Modernity. Only then the constitutional provisions for Equality and Freedom attain fulfillment and realization. Law is the condensed spirit of universal human values of a civilized and democratic society. Law safeguards the legal guarantees by reminding the State of its constitutional duties and liabilities.

The other theme that appears in her writings relates to education. In author's view education is not an end in itself; it has to be a means for social change with social justice. Therefore type of education is more important that education alone. Education that create the feeling and notion of equality, fraternity and brother hood is necessary for working of democracy.

Dr. Priya Rao has brought insights on these issues in a rational and dispassionate manner. She provides a legal perspective for understanding social and political issues. The insights that she brought on Justice to Common man, Protective Discrimination, Woman Empowerment, Education, Child Rights etc. are indeed progressive and relevant. I congratulate Priya Rao for her contribution. It will be useful for researchers, students, common readers and policy makers.

Sukhadeo Thorat
Chairman, ICSSR
New Delhi

Preface

Development cannot be discussed independent of social factors in third world countries, which are characterized by poverty and social inequalities. Development assumes special significance in as much as equality of opportunity and protection to the interests of weaker section, children's and women is concerned. There has always been a conflict between the law and society for the simple reason that the laws made by the government may not be in the interest of every citizen in the country. As a consequence agitations, movements and violent out bursts some times occur demanding relief from laws. Development also includes special concessions or treatment to certain sections such as backward classes, women or children. Development strategies are invariably backed by the force of laws made by a democratically elected government. Hence it becomes an important concern for the government to look after the interests of all citizens including vulnerable groups such as minorities, women or weaker sections.

The political factors in a democracy make a great difference to legislative process. Though it is a parliamentary democracy characterized by parliamentary supremacy it is often observed that it is the ruling party or the dominant party leading the executive that controls the parliament. It is more an executive supremacy rather on than legislative. In many burning issues such as affirmative action for backward classes, women empowerment, electoral reforms or anti corruption laws the ruling party always manages to bring out legislations of its interest, no matter whether the opposition parties accept it or not. Vote bank politics, nepotism, disregard for welfare of common citizens, etc., often happen to be the results of sectarian political interest.

Progress of a nation in terms of economy and society must have empowerment of women as an important component. It is unfortunate that in the last 60 years of independence we have not been successful in emancipating woman of the country from illiteracy and exploitation. Similarly children of the country are another area of serious concern as it happens to be a fact that millions of them are either involved in child labour or illegal trafficking or abused. The U.N. convention on right of children 1986, had resolved to improve the health of children and put an end to exploitation and in human treatment. All the member nations are signatories to this convention. In India though effective legislations were made to prevent exploitation of children and ensure their happy childhood the execution of the laws has not been effective, for we continue to have millions of children's as child laborers even today. It all seems that there exists a contradiction between the intent of the legislature and the execution of the same.

Education is the real investment in the development of a country. We have a lot to learn from China in this regard which has designed a policy of eduction in tune with the *Four Modernisations* theme. Enormous amounts of allocations were made for education in general and higher eduation in particular. We, in India, have been struggling hard to formulate a sound policy since independence. With millions of unemployed youth getting disenchanted with the system it will be a serious problem sooner or later if we do not raise to occasion and address the relevant issues. Education policy has to focus on development of the nation with it's youth as it's agents of change. A national vision must become the driving force. Education leads to imparting of social justice too for it educates people about their rights and liabilities. Equity must go hand in hand with inclusion and expansion. The recommendations of Knowledge Commission ought to be taken in all sincerity and translated into action with out fail.

Women development is a crucial conern for India as there are million of women enslaved in illiteracy and subjugation. Gender budgeting is the trend of the day and as such it must be implemented in States. Education of women leads to their empowerment and therefore there is a great responsibility on the shoulders of the State and society to make this happen. Girl child neglect is a grave concern as it is reflecting on the declining sex ratio in the country. Female festicide is going on uncontrolled despite the enforcement of legislations. We need to awaken the society and initiate campaign for changing age old degenerative mind set of people. Security and empowerment of women can be first step in this direction. Besides, Girl friendly education infrastructure can make a great difference in protecting the adolescent girls.

Ecology and development are two sides of the same coin. Natural disasters take heavy toll with large scale devastation and damage to life and property. Man made disasters are avoidable unfortunate occurrences which are primarily caused by gross negligence of Industries and administrative machinery that is reasonable for the enforcement of laws for safety of human beings. Similarly the rising temperatures in the atmosphere known as the 'global warming phenomenon' is another factor threatening life and property of all across the world. In spite of high talk by the great nations such as US, France, England etc. the sincerity required in reducing the emission levels is conspicuously absent. In the name of Carbon trading the industrialized and advanced countries only involve in an exercise of emitting more and more CO_2 and buying Carbon credits from the less advanced countries. The major culprits for increasing levels of emissions happened to be the westerns countries who show disregard to the protocols in this regard. There is a great need to understand the issues involved in the development of economy while simultaneously preserving the pristine sanctity of mother earth be it water, soil or air.

I find it useful to share of my thoughts and views with readers on many of the issues with regard to development in general and Social Justices in particular. I have tried to analyze the problem from the perspective of law and legislation and tried to make necessary suggestions wherever required. I hope that the book that consists of articles on various topics will be useful to students Journalist and policy makers.

Dr. Priya Rao

1
Justice Delivery System—Accessibility to Common Man

"Justice delayed is justice denied." This is a famous saying usually quoted in common parlance of law. Equally popular is another adage "justice not only be done but it should also be seen to be done." These two sayings are very important for an understanding of jurisprudence of a country with relation to administration of justice to citizens. Law in a sense is the gift of modernity as opposed to anarchy, lawlessness, and tyranny of the tradition. Here modernity can be interpreted as everyone understands, as the golden mean of rationality and secularism as opposed to human bondage, suppression of freedom and liberty which are the dark sides of the Tradition. Tradition in the entire world has given way to Modernity, and as a result, popular concepts such as democracy, human rights, liberty and freedom have been translated into action in almost all parts the world through the instrument of law and legislation. Today, the system of justice has been constitutionally established and mechanisms put into practice everywhere. Principles of natural justice have been embedded in every law made and enacted by the legislature across the world. A common man is no longer insecure, at least in law. He is protected from oppression, rescued from exploitation and rehabilitated by the state in whatever best possible way he could be. Any law, depriving a citizen of his liberty whether providing for punitive or preventive detention, must be strictly construed;[1] and, if the procedure prescribed by the relevant law has not, in fact, been followed by the Executive in the case before the Court, the prisoner must be set free.[2]

Law and Common Man

A Common Man in common parlance is known as any and every citizen who looks up to the State for protection of his life and liberty. People with power, money and connections are not common men; let us call the latter uncommon for the majority happens to be always the former. R.K. Laxman's cartoons truely contain the caricature of a common man as week and helpless. A plethora of laws are in existence in India which are primarily made to impart justice to every citizen. To name a few we might as well begin with the constitution of India, especially with reference to Chapter III the fundamental rights and go on listing various laws such as IPC, CRPC, Evidence Act, which are the bedrock for judicial administration, in as much as description of substantive offences and procedure for trial is concerned. It is remarkable that in less than 60 years of independence, the republic of India has come up a long way and succeeded in securing justice for all its citizens by way of establishing enormous judicial administrative machinery in the country, with the thousands of courts of different jurisdictions along with High Court and the hon'ble Supreme Court as watchdogs of justice and democracy. But the question arises is whether the laws made are truly effective in imparting justice to a common man. In other words, whether the delivery of justice is within the reach of a common man who is illiterate, ignorant and poor. These questions have not yet been answered in the country to the fullest satisfaction of any thinking mind. The increasing number of under trials in lakhs, the intricate and complicated legal procedures, the un-ending syndrome of poverty and illiteracy and the increasing rate of crime all deny an affirmative answer to the above questions.

Let us take stock of the system of judicial administration

or justice delivery mechanism in the country, so that, we can single out the areas causing concern. In the entire country, justice is sought only through an established framework of prosecution or adjudication, managed by the State. Every offence against a person or property, or even against State by a person is tried in a competent court of law after the charge sheet is submitted by the police preceded by investigation. The procedure of trial is vividly described in CRPC mainly for cases of criminal nature and in some other procedural acts with regard to offences of civil nature. Civil Procedure Code is exclusively meant for trial of offences or causes of civil nature. The judiciary has the responsibility to impart justice through a transparent and objective trial based on the merits of the case and strictly in accordance with the procedure laid down by law. Here lies the catch. A common man in need of justice has to go through the entire procedure of legal system right from approaching the police and to the deposing of statement in the court of law. As the law takes its own course and the legal practitioners do play a crucial role exploring the immense possibilities of law in favour of their respective clients and the trial is held on the merits of the case and of course on the strength of witnesses, it cannot always be guaranteed that a common man would surely get relief he is entitled to. For a fair trial the nature of evidence obtained and the nature of safeguards violated are both important as relevant facts.[3] Moreover, our system of jurisprudence is based on the noble humanistic principle that *"let 100 criminals escape, lest an innocent man should be punished."*

The Drawbacks of the Formal Legal System

The law in India is seasoned more by equity and good conscience rather than by strict adherence to the text. Interpretation of law is an exciting intellectual exercise besides lucrative that at times even brilliant advocates love to indulge in with no regard to the interest of a common man or society. They are not to blame for they are committed to the rules of their profession -save the client. It so happens that often the guilty is let go scot-free and the innocent suffer. So what are the defects in the system and how can a common man's access be improved, is a million dollar question. The justice delivery system of the country, it seems, suffers from the following pitfalls :

The Presumption of Law

To begin with, the Law presumes that the common man knows law and is aware of his legal rights and liabilities. It is often said in law that *'mistake of fact is excusable but mistake of law is not'*. In other words, the law presumes that a citizen who is illiterate, poor and ignorant has read all the laws made in the country (may be 100s or 1000s) and it expects from him to act in accordance with law and perform his duties ; the failure of which will tax him with a legal liability for prosecution. It is absolutely unthinkable that a common man is equipped with legal knowledge and the awareness of the intricacies and finer details of the judicial administrative system. It is equally preposterous to expect a common man with a cause of action to instantly approach police and the courts as the system of engaging a counsel is not inexpensive. Presiding Officer or Judge of a Court is not under statutory obligation to be favourably biased towards an illiterate accused and exonerate him backed by compassionate or philanthropic reasoning. He is supposed to be upright and judge the acts of Parties and not their hearts or lives. The common man finds himself helpless often in proving his innocence or establishing his claims for relief *'beyond reasonable doubt'*. So can we conclude that Law is not common man friendly? Unwillingly though, we may.

Inadequacy of Courts

The number of courts established in the country are far disproportionate in terms of the population of the country and the incessant piling up of cases in courts, un-disposed for years, vouches for the fact that the judiciary is over-burdened with litigations. As per the Statement of erstwhile Union Law Minister Mr. H.R. Bhardwaj[4] there is a backlog of cases in various courts, including in the Supreme Court where it has crossed the 48,000 mark. High courts across the country have a backlog of 3.8 million cases more, while the lower courts across the country have a backlog of over 25 million cases. It is precisely the reason why the Legal Services Authority Act is enforced in the country because of which the alternative grievance redressal mechanisms have been brought into operation in all districts of the country which are popularly known as Lok Adalats. However, the Lok Adalats as a whole, though backed by a lofty goal of reducing the litigations, haven't been successful to the extent expected as they were mostly involved in disposing petty cases of claims. According to the Annual Report of the Ministry of Law and Justice for 2003-04, 12.2 lakh cases were settled in about 40,000 lok adalats organized in 2003. Of these, in about 40,970 motor accident cases, compensation of over Rs. 667.60 crore was directed to be paid. The rest comprised matrimonial, petty civil and criminal and land acquisition cases. What these statistics do not reveal is that a litigant in a lok adalat is most likely agreeing to a settled verdict for negative reasons – for avoiding uncertainties, delays and expense in pursuing litigation in courts. Lok adalats cannot be the answer to the need for quality justice. The legal literacy campaign launched in all districts of the country by the judiciary has of course been of great help to a common man for it, at least, could demystify the awesome legal aspects and impart knowledge to common men.

Limited Scope of PILs

The PIL though came in as a sigh of relief it has not been successful in it's avowed objective justice to common man. The 1977 report of the committee of Justices Krishna Iyer and P.N. Bhagwati, both of the Supreme Court, drew up a detailed scheme which envisaged public interest litigation (PIL) as a major tool in bringing about both institutional and law reform even while it enabled easy access to the judicial system for the poor. PIL was meant to overcome the barriers erected by the formal legal system. Any public-spirited person could bring forth a case on behalf of an indeterminate class with a similar grievance. Public Interest Litigation means a legal action including all proceedings therein initiated in a court of law with a purpose of either enforcing a right or seeking a remedy[5]. The Honourable Supreme Court observed that public interest means an act beneficial to public in general. It connotes action necessarily taken for public interest[6].

The requirement of a formal petition, drawn up in legal language, was dispensed with. Any letter or even a telegram addressed to the court would suffice. The court could go on with the case on the basis of the facts, however brief, brought before it as long as the issue was one of genuine public interest. It would appoint *amicus curiae* to present the case before it, appoint commissioners to verify the facts and expert committees to advise on how to deal with matters of a technical nature. However in the past two decades, the response of the judiciary in its PIL jurisdiction has neither been consistent nor satisfactory. The decisions in the recent past in PILs reflect a distinct shift from issues concerning access to justice for the poor to other issues of public interest which at times, on the contrary, conflict with the rights of the poor. For instance, the court orders in the PIL seeking protection of the forest cover has led to the curtailment of the rights of forest dwellers and tribals to access community resources essential for their subsistence. The PIL jurisdiction now needs a new dimension to restore its avowed role in the legal aid movement.

The not so simple Legal Process

The law pre-supposes certain requirements such as jurisdiction of police stations, courts, judicial officers with reference to territory and nature of cases. A common man is supposed to have a knowledge of that. A poor man from a far off village is expected to reach a police station, launch a complaint and go all the way (walk) back to his village. The police looking to the nature of complaint, takes its own time to investigate and then submits a charge sheet, if satisfied, to the court or else is 'pleased' to submit a final report. Once it comes to the court, the role of advocate begins who takes his own time as per the requirements and 'demands' of his profession. The common man could be a complainant or an accused – and in both cases, either the State is involved as prosecutor with it's public prosecutor frowning at the common man or an advocate is involved as a defence counsel to save the accused-again a common man. In majority of the cases, the complainant and the accused both happen to be a common men as around not less than 50% people in the country are below poverty line and crimes originate, philosophically, out of hunger and insecurity (Raskolnikov the hero in Fyoder Dustovisky's *Crime and Punishment* may not be a wrong analogy). In short, the redressal mechanism pre-exists and a common man is supposed to strictly go through that, no matter whether his desire for justice is worth the trouble.

The Precarious system of Prosecution

State is the sole prosecuting agency as per the provisions of many penal laws including IPC in maximum number of offences involving person and property. It is, interestingly, the state which prosecutes the accused and not the common man who is the victim. Surprisingly enough the State can withdraw the prosecution (of course with the permission of the Court), if pleased, against the accused irrespective of the wishes of the Victim—the common man; be it a riot or a case of endangering peace of socity. The prosecution is carried on by the agencies of the State, such as police, district prosecution officer etc. who are supposed to perform the responsibilities with an aim to protect the common man, however, the facts belie such an expectation as majority of cases a prosecution initiated by the State end up in dismissal either for want of evidence or due to witnesses turning hostile over night. How relevant is a system of State run prosecution which ultimately ends up in letting the accused go unpunished is a major concern if the justice delivery system is to be common-man friendly. Transparency and fair play often end-up as cry in wilderness especially in the process of investigation by the police, for it is the police which has the final say in either filing a charge sheet or sending a Final Report. A common man seeking justice cannot keep track of the process of investigation at the cost of his daily bread and family. Illiteracy being the major curse on a sizeable population of the country, it is even hard to imagine that a common man knows how an investigation is conducted. He has to file an application under RTI if he intends to know *who holds the Riffle* and *who fires it* (Nepoleaon). It would only add further tale of woe. The system leaves enough room for subjectivity and prejudice in a process of fact-finding that is in exclusive domain of IO.

The mechanism of justice, in so far as cases of civil nature are concerned, doesn't seem to be any better than it's counterpart – the criminal justice. A common man has to wait for days, weeks, months and years to get his claim settled through the courts. Let us not mention generations to make it sound more gloomy; it is often true though. Extraordinary delays in the adjudication process take away substantially the effect of the relief that a common man is entitled.

Expensive Counselling

The existence of advocates is sine-qua-non in the system of justice delivery for they know law and fight for justice in favour of their clients. Abraham Lincoln said wittingly describing Lawyers;

> *"Discourage litigation. Persuade your neighbours to compromise whenever you can. As a peacemaker the*

lawyer has superior opportunity of being a good man. There will still be business enough." (ThinkExist.com Quotations Online)

Nevertheless, the advocates have a more positive and pro-active role to play in order to help justice being done to the client as per the spirit of the Advocates' Act 1961. But today, it is unfortunate that professionalism has crept into the noble profession of law which originally meant for helping the common man seeking justice. Though the law ensures security, protection and justice to a citizen, it is not such an easy task to receive the same without the help of the learned man - the Advocate. The State has made provisions for legal aid. When the accused is unable to engage a lawyer owing to poverty or similar circumstances, the trial would be vitiated unless the State offers free legal aid for his defence by engaging a lawyer to whose engagement the accused does not object.[7] This right of an indigent accused arises from the moment he is first produced before a Magistrate.[8] It does not require any application from him.[9] Even it is a duty caste up on the State to afford grant-in-aid to recognised private law colleges that turn out law graduates.[10] Despite the legal aid mechanism introduced by the State, a common man has no immediate access to the same for want of procedural requirements such as qualifying income limits, caste certificates etc. Engaging an advocate on one's own is no less expensive affair either. Often it is also true, unfortunately, that majority of advocates are no better than common men as the major chunk of them either hail from or belong to poor families and constantly engage in fending for themselves like honey bees. (Remember the Advocate's act of 1961 provides for relief measure through Bar Councils in fovour of poor advoctes and theisr families.) The uncommon among them are fortunate Queen bees with roaring practice and celebrity status with sufficient leisure at their command to interpret Law before the Dias and gracefully lead the Bar Associations.

Subordinate Legislation – A Necessary Evil

The State makes laws and keep enacting them to counter every situation of injustice in the society. Nevertheless the rule making of an act or a law is not done by the legislature and is left to the purview of subordinate legislation, otherwise known as the Departments of the 'Executive'.

Often the subordinate legislation through rule making power thwarts the spirit and the intent of the legislation and it takes years and years to strike off a particular rule that is ultra vires the parent act or Constitution. It is again only with the intervention of the High courts and the Apex Court. Until then the system is not changed and the justice is not meted out though the legislature never intended so. Still a rule cannot be struck down on the ground that no opportunity was given to be heard to a person affected by such rule.[10]

Unlike the Acts passed by the Legislatures, the rules and regulations made by the Departments of the Govt. or other non-sovereign authorities subordinate can be enforceable unless they are published officially in Gazette and made known to the people affected by them.[11] If it is not published or laid before the Legislature as required the rule must be void.[12] But the question is how many people can access a Gazette? A common man is not even literate enough to read a Gazzette. Also important question is whether the Legislature in a Parliament Supremacy Democracy like ours will adhere to legislative requirements sincerely? It is any body's imagination as how misuse of offices take place. The power of the Executive through the subordinate legislation has become the necessary evil and the Justice Delivery Mechanisms suffer consequentially.

No Expansion of Legal Education

Rule of law is the chief character of modern democratic government though, the tragedy is that a common man does not know what the laws are according to which the governance (rule) is supposed to take effect. No legal education is a part of syllabi of common curriculum for various courses in the country from 10+2 to Masters degree barring law courses such as L.L.B/LL.B/L.L.B. or LLM/ L.L.M./LL.M. Basics parts of law have never been made a part and parcel of either school education or higher education in the country. It is sad that though people are qualified otherwise with professional degrees such as medicine, engineering or humanities they do not have sufficient knowledge of the basic law of the land. The procedure of law and justice delivery system even at the rudimentary level was not made a part of the course in any of the curriculums.

Neutrality to Gender

Women constitute one half of the population and yet there is no expression as 'common woman' there are supposed to seek consolation in the term common man as includes woman too. Gender budgeting is the trend of the day as women constitute 50% of the population ; and they are in a way 'special class of citizens' for they suffer from innumerable situations of discrimination, ill-treatment and in-security. But the law is neutral and impartial to gender, barring a few provisions in few Acts. Women are treated equally with men in law so far as legal liabilities are concerned. Though special laws such as Dowry Protection of women from Domestic Violence Act 2005 are enacted with a view to protect the weaker sex a separate justice delivery mechanism as such is not biased in favour of women at least technically, which it should be in all bonafide. The Constitution, it is note worthy, lays down in Art. 15(3) that Legislature can make special provisions[13] towards protection of women and children.

Marital problems are the commonest manifestations of injustice that looms large on women. Protection of women from Domestic Violence Act 2005 has many provisions for seeking protection from State against In-Laws such for maintenance, care of protection officers and also seek matrimonial home etc. However, it is a pity that majority of women never make use of these legal provisions for the simple reason that they are not aware of them. It is surprising that despite constitutional guarantees of justice, freedom, equality and dignity, sexual abuse and other heinous crime are never ending in the country. A casual look at the media coverage in no way gives relief from the past. On the contrary the picture is more demoralizing besides horrifying. The Law has provisions for protection though, how the cutting edge—the prosecution agency and the Judiciary performs their bit is very crucial in bringing the accused to justice.

Let us briefly refresh ourselves with certain important legal provision for protection of women exclusively.

Section 366 Indian Panel Code deals with kidnapping or abducting a women to compel her to marry against her will or in order that she may be seduced to illicit intercourse, or knowing it to be likely that she will be forced or seduced to illicit intercourse. Sections 373 and 374 Indian penal code deal with buying and selling of minor girls for purposes of prostitution.

A prosecution for sexual harassment under Section 354 Indian Panel Code requires two factors: to be proved:

- that the accused assaulted or used criminal force to a woman.
- that such assault was with an intention or knowledge that it may or is likely to outrage the modesty of the woman.

It becomes extremely difficult to substantiate or prove the above two requirements in hostile environment where a women's modesty and dignity could be at stake. Here lies the necessity of gender preferential soft trial. It was held by hon'ble Supreme Court that any act on the part of the person who lead a women astray from the path of rectitude is said to be seduction, and if it is followed by intercourse it will be seduction for illegal intercours[14]. If the girl is 18 or over she could be abducted not kidnapped but if she was under 18 years she could be abducted as well as kidnapped if the taking was by force or the taking or enticing was by deceitful means[15]. These wise interpretations of the Court may go unheeded by the subordinate judiciary if it is not sensitized towards special nature of charges involving women.

Unemployment and poverty, alcoholism, marital maladjustment, religion and inefficient legal machinery are attributed to crimes against women. Here lies the importance of legal education for women for it can be the real weapon of empowerment to enable them to safeguard themselves. The Legal Services Authorities act (1987) has a to contribute to this end only if the para legal services are truly extended across the territory.

It is unfortunate that the BCI has reduced the upper age limit to 30 years for enrolment in law courses in the country. Though under challenge the idea is impractical and not backed by reason hasty. How can a woman be expected to bear children and also bear qualifications simultaneously before 30. Too unkind a 'cut' off. Equity is what women deserve and Law has it as an integral part of it's entity. Though in principle it is agreed up on by all it appears that it's a long way ahead in its realisation. Let us not forget the landmark judgement of Supreme Court with regard to the rehabilitation of sex workes in four Metros of the Country in *Gaurav Jain vs Union of India*. The Court had directed the State to show compassion to the suffering women in red light areas and ruled that their children be provided with education and health. The spirit of the decision is a path finder for the entire subordinate judiciary.

A Few Remedies to Reflect upon

The above discomfitures in the existing system of delivery mechanism of justice are being serious impediments on way to a quick and fair system of justice these need to be rectified or improved in order to provide a common man centric judicial administration.

The following are some of the areas of intervention by State and civil society that can improved with a view to create an effective legal mechanism to provide justice to a common man and revamp the system of delivery of justice:

Decentralization

Decentralization of adjudication systems is very essential in order to:

(*a*) reduce the workload of the existing courts,

(*b*) to save the time and expenses of a common man and

(*c*) ensure quality of disposal

The Gram Nyayalay concept is a whiff of fresh air which surely would shower, in near future, the benefits of simplified process of adjudication. This Legislation is aimed at establishing a system of judiciary that will be less expensive, free from protracted procedural wrangles, quick and available at the grass-roots level. The new system is also expected to be more accessible to the common man and render justice as enshrined in article 39A of the Constitution. The government will appoint more than 6,000 first class magistrates to preside over mobile gram 'Nyayalayas', or village courts, across the country to establish a quick and efficient system of judiciary at the grass root level.

Institutional Reforms

The existing network of legal services committees require to primarily, initiate law and institutional reform particularly in the context of laws that criminalize the activities of the poor. The practice of insistence on monetary bail bonds and sureties irrespective of the economic status of the accused, for example, needs intervention. Similaraly the functioning of penal custodial institutions that hold vagrants, mentally ill, sex workers and women and children in prison-like conditions call for a soul searching exercise to keep things in place.

The task of aiding the enforcement of existing laws is also very essential. For example the demeaning practice of manual scavenging of dry latrines is still in practice notwithstanding the existence of a law (1993) prohibiting it. Similarly Female infanticide, child prostitution, child labour, have all been prohibited by enacted law but flourish in society. Unless the State takes the responsibilty to enact laws strictly justice will be a far cry for the victims, no matter how many courts establish and how many officers notified to adjudicate.

Reaching legal services to the community is a priority if we are committed towards adressing the legal needs of the poor and week. The Legal services committees need to act working on the pattern of neighbourhood law offices. With community participation the committees could be located in the community and engage services of proffesssional lawyers and of those service providers of related disciplines. Coordination with other agencies including the government offices, police, the courts and the various commissions would become easier with the facilitative role of these proffessional. They could take help of lawyers or paralegals to visit govt. offices, police stations, prisons or other custodial institutions to assess the need of legal assistance to the aggrieved. There can be better interface between the institutions and the people in need of protection or counselling.

Basically, the formal legal system must admit the fact that as long as the basic needs of the socially, educationally and economically weaker sections are not resolved, they are unlikely respect the stuctural frame of judicial system. The consequences will lead to faith in extra legal (often illegal) ways of seeking justice or rather in private justice.

Community Specific Adjudication Systems

India being a country with more diversity than unity, community-specific redressal mechanisms independent of established law may be encouraged. The Vth Schedule (Art. 244) provides constitutional arrangements to this effect. The Governors are empowered to exempt any Act either of Union or of State in this context. For instance, community-specific customs and practices prevalent in tribal groups and other social groups may be given due place in the established formal system of justice with elaborate provisions for appeal in the event of disagreement. Unified Code of Law is of course an acceptable proposition, but however, the existing differences of human social behaviour based on age-old practices cannot be overlooked. The need of the hour is to make room for separate systems of justice in tune with diverse social fabric of the country. It is a fact that some of such systems exist such as *Shariat*, or special provisions for *Kachhi Memons of Gujarat*, etc. It needs more expansion which in other words means more inclusion. The existing procedural rigmarole and voluminous paper work in the courts may be reviewed and common-man friendly simple procedures with greater accessibility introduced instantly.

The Positive Role of Bar vis a vis the State

The legal profession has a unique human responsibility of imparting justice to clients and as such it is expected that the learned advocates do not involve in professionalism rather than dedicating themselves to the tenets of august profession of law i.e. justice to the innocent. Frequent adjournments and prolonged trials can be cut-short or avoided with a positive determination of the Bar. The responsibility of the Bar as the treasure of the legal knowledge is manifold. Learned advocates should organise citizen-friendly camps for legal education and hold frequent seminars for dissemination of ideas and for kindling the light of law and justice in the minds of common man. They should always be in constant interaction with the State and appeal to the subordinate legislation to check the rules that are ultra vires to the parent statutes or to the Constitution.

The Lok Adalats and legal services have more pro-active and result oriented job to be performed in relation to the requirements of justice. Frequency of Lok Adalats has to be increased and alternative dispute resolving mechanisms given more importance. State must allocate sufficient budget to meet the needs. Women and children are a *special class of citizens* under Article 15(3) of the Constitution specially makes it the duty of the State to look after them. The State should make women and child-friendly laws and procedures with a positive bias in their favour for they are *special class of citizens* and are a part of a common man.

Bar can sensitize the State (Government) towards spreading citizen benefiting information. Publication and distribution of basic legal concepts and laws including Rules of Business by which government functions is very essential as it disseminates knowledge. Department of Education and Department of Public Relations may be pulled in to engineer a campaign towards this purpose. Sufficient financial allocations can made to Bar Councils to spearhead the mission. Accessibility literature in vernacular medium would further results in the miraculous awakening of stakeholders at the receiving end. This will reduce the work load of Information Commissions. State must realise the importance of this aspect.

Legal Literacy and Legal Education in Curriculum

Legal education in one form or the other to such an extent of imparting basic knowledge of law and justice delivery system can be introduced right from school education to higher education, with the sense of proportion. This would help proliferation of legal knowledge which would result in turn in protection of common man. Right from the middle school standard i.e., eighth standard onwards, the basic concepts of three major acts i.e., Indian penal code, criminal procedure code, Indian evidence act can be taught especially to the girl students in all the schools as a part of curriculum. The content of basic legal education can be phased out up to graduation on a compulsory basis no matter what the regular faculty involved in, is.

The legal literacy course of this nature can be of a qualifying nature with a bearing on the total aggregate of marks just as it is, in the case of languages. Practical exposure to court proceedings, police stations procedures, can be incorporated at the level of matriculation and higher secondary certificate examinations. This would help demystify the unwanted awe and fear of the uniform services (police). Special sessions on important case studies, leading cases on women issues can be conducted in order to instill confidence courage at practical level. Short term courses on basic legal knowledge can be conducted for working women irrespective of their nature of employment.

The above are some of the solutions the State may seriously take note of and start acting positively. The legal luminaries both from Bench and Bar have a lot to contribute in the endless endeavour.The Common man is ubiquitous in the society and he or she is the force behind the existence of a Democratic system of governance. The faith and trust of Common man in the system of justice is very essential to provide a rationale for the very existence of Judiciary or even the State for that matter. It will be very difficult the day it is lost.

REFERENCES

1. Kishori Mohan Bera v. State of W.B., Air 1972 SC 1749 : (1972) 3 SCC 845; Bhutnath Mate v. State of W.B., AIR 1974 SC 806 : (1974) 1 SCC 645.
2. Naranjan v. State of Punjab, AIR 1952 SC 106 (29) : 1952 SCR 395.
3. State of Punjab vs Baldev Singh, (1999) 6 SCC172 (paras 45 and 57); AIR 1999 SC 2378.

4. Saturday, January 17, 2009 7:50:54 PM by IANS (www.thaindian.com).
5. Janta Dal Vs H.S. Choudhary, AIR 1993, SC 893.
6. Baburam Verma Vs State of U.P., (1971 Lab Lj 235 All).
7. Hussainara Khatoon v. State of Bihar, AIR 1979 SC 1369 (paras 6-7) : (1980) 1 SCC 98; Hoskot Madhav Hayawadanrao v. State of Maharashtra, AIR 1978 SC 1548 (paras 11-13, 24): (1978) 3 SCC 544;
8. Khatri v. State of Bihar, AIR 1981 SC 928 (para 4) : (1981) 1 SCC 635.
9. Suk Das v. Union Territory of Arunachal Pradesh, AIR 1986 SC 991 : (1986) 2 SCC 401: 1986 (2) Crimes 40.
10. State of Maharashtra vs Manu bhai Pragji Vashi, (1995) 5 SCC 730 (para17); AIR 1996 SC1.
11. Trivedi and sons, D.K. VS State of Gujarat, (1986) 2 UJSC 301 (para 50): AIR 1986 SC 1323 : 1986 Supp. SCC 20.
12. Harla vs State of Rajastan, (1952) SCR 110 : AIR 1951 SC 467; Hukum Chand Mills vs State of Madhya Bharat, AIR 1964 SC 1329(1332): 1964(6)SCR857.
13. Balaji,M.R. vs State of MysoreAIR 1963 SC 469:1963 supp.(1)SCR, 439; Case book, pp. 124-25, 130.
14. Ratinarayan Vs. State, 1992, Criminal Law journal, 269, 273, 273.
15. See also, Khalandar Saheb Re, AIR 1955 SC 39.

2
Human Rights and Rights of Children in India

Human rights are those natural rights to human beings recognized by society at large irrespective of any political system. These rights are basically Right to one's life, Right to liberty and Right to property. These rights in short, provide meaning to the very existence of a human being. It is worthwhile to recollect the famous words of Karl Marx "the consciousness of an individual is determined by his social existence and his social existence is not determined by his consciousness." The theory of natural rights emerged in the world as a result of a prolonged struggle for freedom and liberty across the globe. The Magna Carta of England was the first real victory of people towards human rights in 1215 A.D. It provided assurances against arbitrary arrest and also that the king could not impose the taxes without the consent of the people. This is the beginning of the modern voting on Budget in the legislature. The American declaration of independence in 1776 claims "We hold these truths to be self-evident that all men are created equally". The Right to Equality has been recognized as a right in this declaration. This is followed by "Declaration of Rights of Man" signed after the French Revolution in 1789. The Declaration asserts men are all free and equal in all respects thereby emphasizing the lofty principles of liberty, equality and fraternity. The famous slogan of French Revolution "Breath or Blood" against Louis XIV is nothing but the unanimous demand for life and food which is in other words the outcry for right to life as a human right. It is in 1948 after the Second World War which has been a witness to inhuman and cruel subjugation, anti-Semitism and mass-killings in the name of the race the universal declaration of human rights occurred. This declaration is a genesis for the basic human rights which has been in almost all written constitution of the world. U.N. General Assembly adopted the declaration on 10th December 1948 elaborating various civil, political, economic, cultural and social rights as well. Declaration contains 30 articles in which article 1 and 2 sum-up the basic spirit of the rights. For, they say "all human beings are born free and are equal in dignity and human rights without distinction of race, colour, sex, language, religion, political or above opinion.

Rights of Children

The human rights are natural rights available to all without any discrimination. The rights are concerned without consideration of basic life and liberty. The Constitution of India, perhaps the first in the world, to incorporate almost entirely the spirit of the declaration in chapter III by way of providing basic rights of life and liberty (article 21) equality (article 14), prohibiting discrimination in the name of caste, race etc. (article 15, 16). Though human rights have been recognized across the world as sacrosanct and as dictate of reason to be enforced a special emphasis on children hasn't been made in them probably for obvious confidence that children are under the protectorate and care of the parents. It is after four decades that the need for a declaration of child rights has taken shape and got materialised in the form of convention of basic rights of a child under the leadership of United Nations in 1989. As it is said, "child is the father of man." The Convention incorporated full range of human rights - civil, cultural, economic, political and social rights, and made it legal binding internationally. The Convention sets out these rights in 54 articles and two Optional Protocols. It spells out the basic human rights that children everywhere have : the right to survival; to develop to the fullest; to protection from harmful influences, abuse and exploitation; and to participate fully in family, cultural and social life. The four core principles of the Convention, are non-discrimination; devotion to the best interests of the child; the right to life, survival and development; and respect for the views of the child. Every right spelled out in the Convention is inherent to the human dignity and harmonious development of every child. The Convention protects children's rights by setting standards in health care; education; and legal, civil and social services.

Childhood Robbed

By agreeing to undertake the obligations of the Convention (by ratifying or acceding to it), national governments have committed themselves to protecting and ensuring children's rights and they have agreed to hold themselves accountable for this commitment before the international community. States parties to the Convention are obliged to develop and undertake all actions and policies in the light of the best interests of the child. But the tragedy seems to be speaking in as much as the state of child rights across the world is concerned in today's context. Millions of children make their way through life impoverished, abandoned, uneducated, malnourished, discriminated against, neglected and vulnerable. For them, life is a daily struggle to survive. Whether they live in urban centres or rural outposts, they risk missing out on their childhood – excluded from essential services such as hospitals and schools, lacking the protection of family and community, often at risk of exploitation and abuse.

For these children, childhood as a time to grow, learn, play and feel safe is, in effect, meaningless. The startling figures and facts of exploitation of children across the globe are as under:

Trafficking of Children[1]

As per the report of the UNICEF, "The state of the world's children – 2006" 12,00,000 children are becoming victims of trafficking in the entire world whereas 6,00,000 children are subjected to illicit activities. More pathetic situation is that 18,00,000 children are drawn into prostitution and pornography while 3,00,000 children have become victims of armed conflicts across the globe. The worst scenario is that 57,00,000 children are subjugated to forced and bonded labour. All these forms of labour correspond to those outlined in article 3 of the I.L.O Convention no. 182.

Forced Child Marriages[2]

As per International Labour Organisation, "A global alliance against forced labour", ILO Geneva, 2005. 2% out of forced commercial sexual exploitation are men and boys. Many women before they could attain 18 years were married off against their consent in developing countries. The syndrome is more appalling in rural areas than in urban. In sub-Saharan Africa, it is 48% whereas rest and Central Africa, it is 56%. In South-East Asia, it is 54% and even in Latin American and Carribbean it is 31%. In all the developing countries excluding China 45% children are married off before 18 years while the percentage is 57% in the least developed countries.

Orphaning[3]

The state of orphaned children under age 18 in sub-Saharan African, Asia and Latin America and the Caribbean is worse. Under the age of 18, in sub-Saharan Africa, 12.3% of children are orphaned whereas in Asia, they are 7.3% as per the figures of year 2003. In Latin America and Caribbean it is 6.2% of the children orphaned. However, it is interesting to know that in Asia and Latin American countries, percentage of orphaned children is on the decrease in relation to the year 1990 to the extent of 2%

whereas in sub-Saharan Africa, it is on the rise to 2% chronologically.

Child Labour[4]

The phenomenon of child labour in the developing world seems to be never ending. In sub-Saharan Africa, 34% of female children and 34% of male children are involved in child labour, whereas in South Asia, it is 15% and 14%. However in West and Central Africal it is the highest with 45% in each category. A child is considered to be involved in child labour activities under the following classification :

(a) children 5 to 11 years of age that during the week preceding the survey did at least one hour of economic activity or at least 28 hours of domestic work;

(b) children 12 to 14 years of age that during the week preceding the survey did at least 14 hours of economic activity or at least 42 hours of economic activity and domestic work combined.

The Exploitation of Children in India[5]

Ministry of Women and Child Development published a report on Child abuse in India in 2007 where in it is stated clearly that there are different kinds of abuse in young children, in the 5-12 year group, who are most at risk of abuse and exploitation. The details are as under:

Physical Abuse

1. Two out of every three children were physically abused.
2. Out of 69% children physically abused in 13 sample states, 54.68% were boys.
3. Over 50% children in all the 13 sample states were being subjected to one or the other form of physical abuse.

4. Out of those children physically abused in family situations, 88.6% were physically abused by parents.
5. 65% of school going children reported facing corporal punishment i.e. two out of three children were
6. Victims of corporal punishment.
7. 62% of the corporal punishment was in goverment and municipal school.
8. The State of Andhra Pradesh, Assam, Bihar and Delhi have almost consistently reported higher rates of abuse in all forms as compared to other states.
9. Most children did not report the matter to anyone.
10. 50.2% children worked seven days a week.

Sexual Abuse

1. 53.22% children reported having faced one or more forms of sexual abuse.
2. Andhra Pradesh, Assam, Bihar and Delhi reported the highest percentage of sexual abuse among both boys and girls.
3. 21.90% child respondents reported facing severe forms of sexual abuse and 50.76% other forms of sexual abuse.
4. Out of the child respondents, 5.69% reported being sexually assaulted.
5. Children in Assam, Andhra Pradesh, Bihar and Delhi reported the highest incidence of sexual assault.
6. Children on street, children at work and children in institutional care reported the highest incidence of Sexual assault.
7. 50% abuses are persons known to the child or in a position of trust and responsibility.
8. Most children did not report the matter to anyone.

Emotional Abuse and Girl Child Neglect

1. Every second child reported facing emotional abuse.
2. Equal percentage of both girls and boys reported facing emotional abuse.
3. In 83% of the cases parents were the abusers.
4. 48.4% of girls wished they were boys.

The above facts which are admitted by the Government of India itself through the report are alarmingly pathetic. In the light of these, miserable state of children in India, the Protection guaranteed the article 23 and article 15(4), turns out to be a farce. What these articles say is as below :

> ***Article 23*** *(1) : Traffic in human beings and beggar and other similar forms of forced labour are prohibited and any contravention of this provision shall be an offence punishable in accordance with law.*
>
> *(2) Nothing in this article shall prevent the State from imposing compulsory service for public purposes, and in imposing such service the State shall not make any discrimination on grounds only of religion, race, caste or class or any of them.*
>
> ***Article 15 (3) :*** *Nothing in this article shall prevent the state from making any special provisions for women and children.*

This provision as an exception to article 15(1) and (2) which prohibits discrimination on the grounds of religion, race, caste, sex and place of birth. [6] This in other words means that for protection of children positive discrimination can be made. The provisions are for protection and advancement of children. Such special provision, the hon'ble Supreme Court said, may be in the form of reservation.[7] When special reservations to be made in this regard the Court observed that there cn be no limit as to the extent of the reservation with regard to 15(4) or 16(4)[8] Art. 15 (3) must be read harmoniously with Art. 16 to achieve the purpose for which these Articles have been framed[9] Such special provision, it was also observed, may be made either by legislation or by executive order[10] The constitutional provisions are no doubt, exemplary in so far as protection to the children to be accorded by the state is concerned. However, the question remains to be addressed is as to the efficacy of legislations made in tune with these provisions.

It is an irony that despite the enactment of acts such as Child Labour Prohibition Act 1986 and as amended in 2006, and Prohibition of immoral Trafficking Act, the uncontrolled exploitation of young children continues. It is again an area of debate as to the real reason for the failures of the statutes in this context. The enforcement agencies (the state machinery such as Police, Judiciary, Protection Homes) are somewhere lacking in the capacity or in determination in effectively rising to the occasion. Besides it is also possible that the laws made in this regard and the punishments prescribed are suffering from some lacunae due to which the culprits manage to go scot-free.

The National Human Rights Commission in its Annual Report 1999-2000 on page 165, annexure II, comes out with effective recommendations with regard to the protection of children and their rights. Some of the major recommendations of the NHRC are as under :

(a) That the government must ensure full compatibility of its legislation with the Convention on rights of the child.

(b) That the State should take all necessary measures including allocation of required resources (human and financial) to ensure and strengthen the effective implementation of the existing laws.

(c) A comprehensive national plan of action based on Child Rights – an Approach, emphasizing inter-sectoral coordination and cooperation at and between Central, State and Municipal levels of government.

(d) The Commission going further and addressing the social inequalities recommends that in accordance with article 17 of the Constitution, and article 2 of the Convention, the Committee recommends that the State party take steps to ensure states abolish the discriminatory practice of 'untouchability', prevent caste and tribe motivated abuse, and prosecute State and private actors who are responsible for such practices or abuses.

(e) The full implementation of the 1989 Scheduled Castes and Scheduled Tribes (Prevention of Atrocities) Act, the 1995 Scheduled Castes and Scheduled Tribes Rules (Prevention of Atrocities) and the 1993 Employment of Manual Scavengers Act.)

(f) In accordance with article 27 of the Convention, the Commission recommends that the State party take appropriate measures to give effect to its commitments made as Habitat II in 1996 regarding children's access to housing.

(g) That the State establishes mechanisms to ensure these children are provided with identity documents, nutrition, clothing and housing.

(h) That the State ensures the full implementation of the 1986 Child Labour (Prohibition and Regulation) Act, the 1976 Bonded Labour (System Abolition) Act and the 1993 Employment of Manual Scavengers Act.

(i) That the State ensures that laws provide criminal and civil remedies, especially in the light of decisions of the Supreme Court in relation to compensation funds for child labourers (M.C. Mehta vs. The State of Tamil Nadu and M.C. Mehta vs. Union of India).

(j) That the State encourages states and districts to establish and oversee child labour vigilance committees, and ensure that a sufficient number of labour inspectors are adequately resourced to carry out their work effectively.

(k) That the State ensure that legislation criminalizes the sexual exploitation of children and penalizes all the offenders involved, whether local or foreign, while ensuring that the child victims of this practice are not penalized. While noting that Devadasi, or ritual prostitution, is prohibited under the law, the Commission recommends that the State takes all necessary steps to eradicate this practice.

The recommendations of the National Human Rights Commission with regard to rights of children in India have to a great extent been translated into action by quite a few legislations in the country. Some of the important recommendations were translated in to action by legislations as under.

Some of the important Legislations:

1. Child Labour (Prohibition and Regulation) Act,1986
2. Prohibition of Child Marriage Act 2006
3. Juvenile Justice (Care and Protection of Children) Act, 2000
4. Factories Act,1954
5. Probation of Offenders Act, 1958
6. Bonded Labour System (Abolition) Act, 1976
7. Bombay Prevention of Begging Act, 1959
8. Immoral Traffic Prevention Act, 1986
9. Commission for Protection of the Rights of the Child Act, 2005

It is also un-denying that the intention of the legislature behind all the enactments is laudably the welfare security and protection of children in the country. However, as the report of the Government of India it self shows the emancipation from exploitation and abuse is a long way to go. This makes us to think about the possible reasons for poor protection of children and explore the areas of concern.

The state in a democratic society is run by the majority of opinion of the people through the government they have chosen. In such a system of governance, an effective and affirmative action for protection of rights of children should not be a Herculean task to be performed especially when the public opinion and the intention of the legislature are in favour of such an action. Therefore, it appears there are serious gaps in the system of executing the laws. Let us explore the reasons for failure of state mechanism and contemplate on how best the protection can be provided.

Secure Rural Incomes

Child is not an independent entity separate from family and parents. The rights of the child, as a matter of fact, have a direct bearing on the rights of the parents be it human rights or fundamental rights. It is futile to expect the rights of the child to be protected when the basic human rights of the parents themselves are at peril for instance, child labour in India is a direct consequence of poor economic existence of the families. The aggregate income of family is used as a common pool to meet the subsistence needs of the family including the children. Children are used often by the parents for mainly domestic labour within the households for assistance to the parents and often this leads to marketing of labour by child with an understandable hope to raise income of the family. Thus child labour is often voluntary than forced. The bottom line is that the economic well being of a family (parents) is more important issue to be addressed before launching a battle against child labour.

The state has responsibility to ensure a sustainable means of living for all its citizens so that they do not have compulsion to send their children to work in hotels, households, or in to hazardous occupations. The state over the last 60 decades has been struggling its best to ensure a decent living for all citizens through rural development programmes and employment generation schemes. Poverty elevation programmes are at the mercy of the Banks who prefer to finance the private sector. Schemes like IRDP (Integrated Rural Development Programme popularly known as Milch Cattle Scheme has been a failure in raising the incomes of the households. This was primarily because the commercial banks though were nationalised had a half-hearted disposition towards the rural poor. Secondly, the state machinery found it convenient involving corruption at grass-root level endangering the very object of the programme.

The employment generation schemes such as Jawahar Rozgar Yojana (JRY), launched in 1980s and 1990s, though intended to provide wage labour to the rural poor, the material component outweighed the labour component. Consequently, the expectations that the wages would enhance the incomes of the poor remained far from realized. In 1990s the Employment Guarantee Scheme was launched on 2nd October, 1993 with hundred days guarantee with wage employment to BPL families only to end up by creation of miniscule rural assets such as Panchayat Bhavans, Anganwadis, earthen roads etc. with high material component. However, in 21st century, the National Rural Employment Guarantee Scheme (NREGS) initiated by the Prime Minister appears to be stable and meaningful. However, it is difficult to explain the large scale exodus of people from villages especially in backward states in search of employment every year after the harvesting of Kharif.

Majority of construction workers in north Indian cities are drawn from this migration labour which is often exploited by the contractors. Hundreds of cases of conscripted labour in brick-kilns in many States were reported involving forced labour by migrating workers. It is a pity that the entire industrial sector today is using human labour as one of the factors of production on par with land, capital and entrepreneurship without concern for basic human life. Though the state has made inter-state migrant labour act and the contract labour act the exploitation by way of poor wages and inhuman living conditions is going unabated across the country. It is again an irony that though India has stringent labour laws which often criticized for discouraging foreign investment, the punishments provided for violation of labour laws is hardly a deterrent. Despite having more than 35 laws with regard to labour welfare, labour in India is exploited in the hands of capitalists.

The above scenario shows that the average incomes of rural folks whether they are living in the village or migrating for livelihood are not substantial to provide decent education, health and protection to their children. Detailed statistical reports need not be given here in support of this conviction for the facts speak for themselves which are often aired in the media. It is anybody's guess in such a situation what could be fate of the rights of children in the country.

Child Friendly Education : A Priority

Education probably is one of the least priority areas of planning in India. As the budgetary allocations in the plan are not commensurate with the needs of millions of children in the country. Though free education is provided for the children, it is not just pedagogic content which can attract a child to the school. On the other hand, the environment of learning, the infrastructure, the security for an average child whose parents cannot afford a private school is very essential. Mid-day meals, free school books might work as a factor of attraction to ensure the enrolment of children. However, the required number of teachers as per the required ratio cannot be ignored. Majority of schools in India at primary level suffer from lack of teaching staff. The state of school buildings is pathetic in most parts of the country. Though the Sarva Shiksha Abhiyan made a tangible difference, yet much is left to be desired. On the contrary, schooling in cities and urban areas has become a prosperous commercial venture in the hands of capitalists. There is a positive relationship between the level of income of parents and the level of schooling for children. Education is the right of a child and yet, the child doesn't have a choice as the economic inequalities play a negative role. The enrolment percentage of youth between 18 to 23 in India to higher education is 8% at national level which is far less in many states. Less than 15% of the 10th pass-outs enrol themselves for undergraduate courses. It is understandable that when the majority of the children at the age of 17 do not enrol themselves for higher education. The Human Resource Development becomes meaningless. Juvenile Delinquency is a direct result of 'DROP OUT' syndrome.

Secular Society with Equality

Society in India is not governed by the principles of equality, caste, region, are some of the major divisive factors in society which have an adverse impact on the human rights of the people. Children are no exception in this regard to. Life and liberty of a child is often endangered by the exploitation in the name of caste or class; it is more often the caste than the class. The caste system in the Indian system has a pervading principle of ascription of duties in the name of birth. Children of so called low caste often experience seclusion, ill-treatment, ostracize in the society. The morale and self-confidence is suffered to such an extent is rocked by the cruel traditions of society. The tradition of India which firmly stands on the pillars of caste and inferior position of women has not given way to modernity. The tradition is expected to be modernised. On the contrary it is the modernity which is getting traditionalised ; such is the resilience of the society even today. The state, though, has initiated protective discrimination the criteria is caste. It is high time that State adopts the class as criteria of identification instead of caste in order to ensure secular fabric of India.

Exploitation of human being in India is not always secular unlike in the rest of the world. It is often related to the social factors such as caste. The children from lower caste especially the Dalits and tribes suffer more and become victims of exploitation in contrast to their counterparts from upper castes. The Human Rights Commission was very correct in laying emphasis and suggest remedial measures in its Annual Report Annexure II, para 11, page 164. The state needs to enact special laws especially for children of these communities to prevent exploitation against them.

A Sensitive Governance

Sensitization of civil servants and state machinery is equally important in the fight against exploitation of children. The NGOs have been of great help surely in spearheading the child rights protection campaign in the country. More support and cooperation from the state machineries to the NGOs is to be ensured breaking away from routine red-tape of the bureaucracy.

The only Department entrusted the task of the children is the Department of the Women and Child Development. It is surprising that more than 30% of the posts of the field staff such as Supervisors in ICDS programmes in most of the states are vacant. The ICDS services (Integrated Child Development Scheme) provided by the State are basically aimed at improving the nutrition levels of the children from 0–6 years and that of pregnant and lactating mothers. There is no scheme to protect a child from exploitation of any kind in the department. The Juvenile Justice Homes are run by the Social Welfare Department basically cater to the children who are in conflict with law. This is more an aberration than normal positive action. The positive action is more preventive in nature because the children need to be protected before they are exploited and fall in wrong ways. There is a need for separate Ministry and a Department for protection of child rights so that focus can be on the protection of child rights and on the preventive measures connected therewith. The Ministry of Labour is of course doing its bit with the enactment of Prevention of Child Labour Act, nevertheless a holistic approach to the protection of child rights is the need of the hour.

Child Budgeting

Child Budgeting though has taken off in the planning of resources the desired emphasis on areas of serious concern and proportional allocations is yet to take place. For instance the below chart shows the misjudged priorities;

Chart 1-Trend of Expenditure on Children- Union Budget

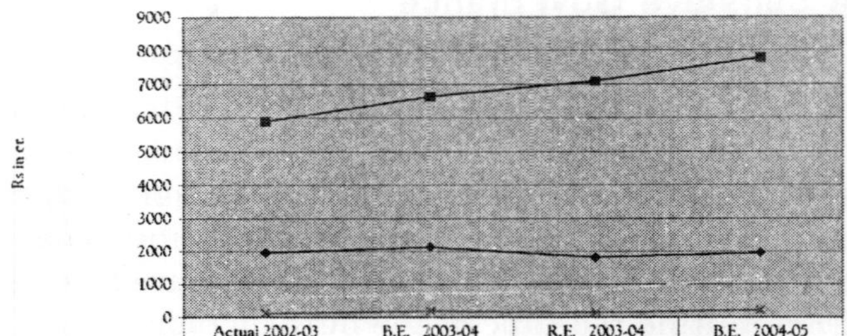

	Actual 2002-03	B.E. 2003-04	R.E. 2003-04	B.E. 2004-05
Child Development and Nutrition	1949.77	2128.61	1808.94	1955.2
Education	5905.55	6637.2	7089.59	7780.8
Health	570.52	727.22	789.61	1214.38
Child Protection and Others	134.92	189.42	148.89	221.76

(Coutesy: www.wcd.nic.in)

The table shows that the allocations for Child protection are the least (221.76 cr) in the year 2005 while it should have been the most in view of increasing trend of exploitation of children. Similarly the allocations for nutrition are also not reasonable especially with around 47% children malnourished in the country. Rather they are constant between 2003 and 2005.

The Government of India has introduced the concept of gender budgeting in the plan process directing all Departments to incorporate the areas of thrust and priority for women with adequate allocation of resources. However, with regard to the child budgeting, the same emphasis doesn't seem to have taken off the ground. For instance, areas like child friendly road facilities, building specifications, public transport arrangements, hospital ambience or infrastructure etc. have not been given enough priority. There is no child budget based audit procedure in many Departments which as a matter of fact is imperative in order to monitor the state of child rights in the country. As children have an important place in the nation building, it is a sine-qua-non that spending from the public exchequer must have a necessary component of budgeting exlusively for them. Or else, it will only be a 'trickle down philosophy' of development that we have to satisfy ourselves with in this area too.

The Integrated Child Protection Scheme (ICPS)

Government of India has recently declared ICPS as a new integrated approach to the problems of children in India. The Government of India has introduced the scheme in the entire country with an MOU with all state govts. It is a compulsory programme with adequate funds allocated to all States with guidelines for State level operations and District level implementation. The idea is to rescue children that are in conflict with Law or in need of care and protection with help of NGOs and State machinery and rehabilitate. Like the *Juvenile Justice Act, 2000* the ICPS defines vulnerability in two categories: children in need of care and protection and children in conflict with law.

Children in need of care and protection is defined as a child who :

(a) Doesn't have a home or shelter and no means to obtain such an abode.

(b) Resides with a person(s) who has threatened to harm them and is likely to carry out that threat, harmed other children and hence is likely to kill, abuse or neglect the child.

(c) Is mentally or physically handicapped, or has an illness, terminal or incurable disease and has no one to provide and care for him/her.

(d) Has a parent or guardian deemed unfit or unable to take care of the child.

(e) Is an orphan, has no family to take care of him/her, or is a runaway or missing child whose parents cannot be located after a reasonable search period.

(f) Is being or is likely to be sexual, mentally, emotionally or physically abused, tortured or exploited.

(g) Is being trafficked or abusing drug substances.

(h) Is being abused for unthinkable gains or illegal activities.

(i) Is a victim of arm conflict, civil unrest or a natural disaster

The new scheme ICPS certainly is endowed with all the required commitments for safety and protection of children that in conflict with nature and need care and protection. This is launched in the year 2009-10 across the country and all states has been compulsorily made partners through special MOU signed. We hope that this programme would yield results substantially in addressing serious problems of exploitation against children if only the state machinery and NGOs connected with the implementation part sincerely discharged their part.

Conclusion

We have discussed various aspects of exploitation and abuse of children across the world and in India as well and tried to find out some of the areas that need special initiative and intervention. In spite of having well-drafted laws intending to protect the rights of the children, it appears that the law hasn't been successful in delivering the results. This is not purely because of either legal lacunae or in-sincere delivery mechanism of the state. Often the symptoms, it seems, are mistaken for the disease. Law is only punitive in nature for it punishes the guilty for violation and thereby works as deterrent against crime. It has rarely a rehabilitative content. Crimes originate from the socio-economic conditions of any given society. Because *'Consciousness of an individual is determined by the social existence'* (Karl Marx). As long as the circumstances that give birth to crime persist, it is difficult to eradicate the criminal tendencies. Therefore, a holistic approach for wholesale social engineering is very essential for a society like India where inequalities and exploitation go hand-in-hand. Poverty, disease, unemployment, illiteracy, inequalities based on caste or religion have to be addressed primarily so that an environment of equality, security and welfare of all can be ensured. Children being part of the society, cannot be subjected to all the maladies and miseries of the system at large.

It is the human beings i.e. adults who need education towards modernity as opposed to tradition. It is education in true sense which can usher in a revolution with equality, freedom and economic security for all in the society which includes children too. It is however, not to discourage the parallel efforts of the state and individuals that are aimed at rescuing the children from exploitation and abuse. These efforts have,in their own right, a strong deterrent effect on the tendencies for exploitation of children and more and more support and help needs to be extended from everyone in the society. Nevertheless, one should not turn a blind eye to the fact that protection of child rights cannot be seen in isolation from protection of rights of citizens in general which includes parents.

The exploitation and abuse what is prevalent against children as we have seen from the data, is one facet of attack on humanity and human beings in general ; millions of people across the world are equally subjected to exploitation, humiliation and abuse in one form or the other. It is worth recollecting the famous judgement of Supreme Court with regard to red light areas in *'Gaurav Jain vs. Union of India'* case. The Honourable court spoke out its heart in favour of protection for lakhs of unfortunate women (Prestitutes) and their children. Consequently, the government of India has come up with reasonable measures of protection.

Today, exploitation of poor and helpless human beings is continuing either in the name of caste or in the name of class. These are larger issues to be addressed which have a direct bearing on the rights of the child as well. Protection of child rights only ends up as wild geese chase if the basic human rights of the people are not protected in the first instance. Though it is not exactly saying 'putting the cart before the horse', yet, action requires to be initiated simultaneously. Obviously even if a child is rescued from abuse or exploitation, it cannot be guaranteed that he or she does not go back into the same hell when the parents are not in a position to provide the required security. Thus it is a larger arena of activity involving the human rights and rights of child that need to be taken into account before arriving at any conclusion.

With the onset of 21st century, the communication revolution with a powerful electronic media, the state of affairs seems to be certainly looking up. We can hope for better protection of human rights and rights of child today than what we could have a few decades ago. Let us sum up with the quote from the document *'A world fit for children'* para 4 of UNICEF,

"We reaffirm our obligation to take actin to promote and protect the rights of each child – every human being below the age of 18 years, including adolescents. We are determined to respect the dignity and to secure the well-being of all children..."

REFERENCES

1. (*Every Child Counts : new global estimates on Child Labour ILO*, International Programme on Elimination of Child Labour, Statistical Informational Programme on Child Labour, April 2002.)
2. (Multiple indicator cluster surveys (MICS) Demographic and Health Surveys (DHS) and other national service).
3. *A Joint Report of new orphan estimates and a framework for action, UNAIDS / UNICEF / USAID, New York, July, 2004.)*

4. *Multiple indicator cluster surveys (MICS) and Demographic and Health Service (DHS) and other national service*
5. *Study on Child Abuse in INDIA 2007 Ministry of Women and Child Development Government of India:)*
6. Dattaraya Motiram More v/s State of Bombay, AIR 1953 BOM. 311
7. (Toguru Sudhakar Reddy v. Govt. of A.P. AIR 1994 SC 544 (para 3) : 1993 Supp. (4) SCC 439.
8. Ibid, (para 3) : 1993 Supp. (4) SCC 439)
9. Govt. of A.P. v. P.B.Vijaykumar, (1995) 4 SCC 544 (para 3) : 1993 Supp. (4) SCC 439).
10. Balaji M.R v. State of Mysore, AIR 1963 SC 649 : 1963 Supp. (1) SCR 439; Casebook pp.124-25, 130)

3

Examination : A Process of Learning

The position paper on examination reforms by national focus group of NCERT Delhi (*First Edition Mach 2006 Chaitra 1928)* makes thought provoking recommendations with regard to required changes to be made in the system of examinations in India. Though the focus was on Higher Secondary examinations the thrust underlying has a direct bearing on higher education sector too. Let us quote some relevant suggestions as back ground for the topic:

Now, with computerization of registration and grade reporting, it is possible to present a wider range of performance parameters on the mark sheet – absolute marks/grades, percentile rank among all candidates of that subject, and percentile rank among peers (e.g. schools in the same rural or urban block.) The last parameter, in particular, we believe to be a crucial test of merit. Making this information public will allow institutions of higher learning to take a more complex and relativist view of the notion of merit.

The practice of forcing teachers to examine is highly unlikely to lead to good examining and should be abandoned forthwith. Furthermore it should be recognized that all good teachers do not make consistent examiners and vice versa. If boards pay examiners better – and we recommend a rise in daily wage from the low Rs 100 or 125 per day by a factor of two or three here, not 10% or 20% more – and weed out poorly motivated examiners many of the core problems will get solved.

Paper-setting needs drastic reform. In fact, as has been successfully tried in Maharashtra (though for reasons of security rather than quality) the focus should shift to question-setting from paper-setting. It should not be necessary that individual questions are written by experts. Good questions should be canvassed around the year from teachers, college professors in that discipline, educators from other states, and even students. These questions, after careful vetting by experts should be categorized according to level of difficulty, topic area, competency being evaluated, and usage and testing record, and drawn on.

A sensitive teacher usually picks up the unique strengths and weaknesses of students, one should utilize her insight in assessment and empower her, by empowering the system of internal assessment.

The recommendations have a solid thrust on reforming the methods of conducting written examination. Written examination is ofcourse the sine-qua-non for a meaningful process of learning, be it a formal coarse of learning or informal. There has been a lot of debate in the country for quite some time with regard to need for reforms in the Examinations. The subject of debate being too vast, it is practically not practical to rope in all aspects of it. I will confine myself to the area of written examination and the need for certain reforms there in. It will be prudent at the outset to understand what an examination means to the student and to the teacher.

Written Examinations : Objectives and Ingredients

Examination is often perceived as a challenge in arena for a Gladiator who has only one choice; either kill or get killed. Examination in Indian scenario, at least, is a nightmare, a hurdle to cross, or in other words a crisis to riddle out of. Often students take shelter in divine blessings by way of taking vows to shave their heads, if they pass in first class. They normally visit temples just before exams and make offerings to secure divine interventions. The mothers do also join them by fasting to please Gods to help their children. Television is turned off for a month till the exams are over. During Exams quite a few students wear the sacred pendants of Gods, good luck looms etc. Some even go to the extent of choosing the wardrobe for luck. The entire atmosphere gets charged with tension, fear and seriousness causing sleepless nights. The basic mission is to get through the exam in one way or the other. The day the exams are over it will be an occasion for celebration and fun irrespective of the prospects of results. The entire saga of exam happens to be more a marathon race than a process of learning. This in no case be called examination.

Examination in my view is an essential phase of learning. It is more a revision of what one has leant rather than what one has memorised without knowing the meaning. In other words it should be a test of what is understood than what is remembered or memorised by heart. The ideal examination must have the following objects and content:

(*a*) Inspiration to express ones knowledge of subject by various methods of examinations, such as term papers, class room participation, unit tests etc.

(*b*) Student friendly method of extracting what one has learnt

(*c*) Absence of *win / lose* restrictions

(*d*) Performance parameters to grade students in place of Topper –Pauper evaluations.

(*e*) The examination must be a continuous process of learning like in semester method.

(*f*) Participation of students in the role of teachers with mock class-room situations.

(*g*) Questions based on analytical techniques than mere reproduction of memorised answers.

The above objects and ingredients in a system of examination will have encouraging effects on students to learn in place of reading texts. The examination will no longer remain a nightmare or a challenge to prove oneself as against others. Let us discuss in detail the above components:

Inspiration to express ones knowledge

Student needs to be inspired to learn sincerely in place of merely attending the classes for the sake of admission card (hall ticket). The desire for knowledge or the curiosity for knowing the unknown is an inborn trait of every human being. As Michel Angelo the famous Italian Sculptor, once replied to a question as to how he makes beautiful statues, *'the rock already contains the statue. It is only a matter of extraction'* every student has the innate desire to learn. It is only a matter of right method of teaching that makes him learn. Examination is also a method of teaching for, it trains him to answer question with precision and clarity which is possible only if one has learnt the subject. The pattern of examination must be such that student is inspired to express what he learnt. This is only possible by designing a system of testing the knowledge which creates an interest in the examinee in place of fear. A method of passing or failing an examinee is the worst ever form of test for, it creates insecurity in the mind of the student with the domicile's sword hanging over his head. Inspiration is generated when a relative marking for various areas of knowledge is designed with a view to ensure that the student will not fail except in the worst case. System of written examination should consist of various parts in the question paper to give a ropeway so that student can make-up for the drawbacks in one area with another. Objective type questions with MCQ, short answer type questions, matching of answers etc. will instil confidence in the student in the examination hall in attempting to answer the questions. Question papers only with essay type questions make the examination, a boring exercise as the system of writing answer is similar for each question. Secondly, student finds it convenient to write anything and get away with a hope that the examiner might turn a blind eye to some of his answers and award marks. Often this hope is not un-justified.

In addition to the above pattern of question papers for written examination, we need to have a participatory approach towards examination by way of dividing the assessment through unit tests, term papers, group discussions etc. Term papers will keep the student on the toes always for, he has to be prepared to re-produce what he has learnt by way of a term paper in fixed intervals. This makes the student to learn continuously and revise frequently to make himself ready to face the tests. As term papers are common to all student in a class, a competitive spirit develops in the mind that works as a catalyst towards continuous preparedness. Unit tests are the other form of evaluating the student in frequent intervals in a examination hall scenario, though the results of the unit tests are not added in the final aggregate examinations. These tests lead to the preparedness of the student without the eleventh hour hurry-worry. It will be prudent to include the results of the unit tests in the aggregate marks of the final examination provided the management of the academic institutions contemplate in such direction.

Participation of students in pedagogic exercise along with the teachers in a class-room situation, in a way, is the best method of teaching and examining a student. Teaching has unfortunately become a one-sided soliloquy in a theatrical manner in most of the institutions. It often works as an effective sedative to the student to steal a nap at the back benches. Special sessions need to be organized for class-room discussions alongwith faculty members on issues and topics that are crucial for understanding the subject as a whole. As the group mentality is different from that of individual, every student is encouraged to contribute his best and learn a bit during the course of discussions. The assessment of students can be taken up during the class-room discussions and evaluation can be made in the most transparent and objective manner.

Student Friendly Methods

In a traditional system of examination, students are put on tenterhooks for routine formalities and red-tape such as showing of hall-ticket, leaving books, slips, papers outside the examination hall, prohibition to talk to other examinees etc. A student is more seen as a potential criminal in the hall even without an evidence of either his nature to do so or his intention towards resorting to illegal means. Surprise inspection squads make matters even worse by literally frisking the student in the event of any doubt or apprehension. Students including those who have prepared well for the exam get tens and insecure during the squad inspection in an examination hall, resulting in confusion and sudden loss of memory of what they have learnt. This leads to disorganized writing of answers or even missing out the relevant points of presentation. Mistrust towards a student is nothing but a mistrust of the teaching system of institution. Suspecting students with an apprehension of use of unlawful means in the examination hall is disgraceful and is against the dignity of a fellow human being. As the lofty principle of law says, *"let hundred criminals escape, lest an innocent should be punished."* for the sake of few delinquent students that resort to unlawful means, it is not reasonable or human to suspect every student in an examination hall.

Formalities such as admission cards, roll numbers, signatures, entry of details in answer-sheet have a tendency to dilute the concentration during the examination. If these formalities are required, they might as well be completed after the examination is over. Minimum formalities would lead to delivery of maximum output that a student has. Restricting students from communicating with fellow students is an unreasonable prohibition for the simple reason that a student cannot copy an answer in such a brief communication which might not necessarily be intended towards such an end. On the contrary, restriction free atmosphere in the examination hall, makes the student mentally free and confident to write whatever best he can.

Absence of Win/Lose Restrictions

Examination happens to be the logical culmination of an academic session for a particular course. It is often experienced that institutions lay down stringent rules as qualifications to take an examination. These rules are so pervasive as to engulf the entire process of learning right from taking admission, till submission of examination form. For instance, affixing photographs, signatures, payment of fees through bank drafts or treasury challans, submission of forms in fixed counters, fixed attendance etc. frighten the student with fear of foregoing an opportunity to sit for the examination in the event of any lapse in the entire process. As if it isn't enough that the students are expected to collect their hall-tickets, produce no-dues certificate, and deposit books back to library just before the examinations. An average student is bogged down by these *'do'* and often fails to pay sufficient attention to revision of the subject. The formalities such as the above, though necessary, need to be rationalised or moderated to give minimum strain to a student at the nick of time. When a student has registered himself for a course, he is assumed to take the examination and pass through. Demanding a variety of compliance and adherence to un-productive restrictions makes no sense for, the ultimate result is the certificate/degree that he is expected to receive from the institution subject to his eligibility. Any technical lapses on the part of student can always be rectified or made-up before awarding the degree or certificate.

Secondly, attendance is the most traditional method of ensuring the presence of a student in a class. In other words, it is a prison like situation where the guards ensure the inmates of jail to be around under surveillance or observation. *Whether the attendance in a class-room ensures the learning of the student or, is it the learning content and teaching technique that ensures attendance is a million dollar question.* A student is not permitted to sit for an examination when his attendance falls short of required number of days, no matter whether he has learnt something or not. *If attendance is the only yardstick of learning, then, all the students who attended sufficiently should pass the examination. But unfortunately it doesn't happen so. This means that there is no relation between attendance and qualifying an examination. The worst is even when the pass marks are kept at 33%, still, more than 50% students who attended the classes fully, fail in the examinations.* This throws light on the fact that an examination should be independent of attendance in the class-room because it creates a win-lose situation for a student at the very preliminary stage. It will not be a bad idea to do away with the attendance altogether I may sound *Heretic* though.

Failing in an annual examination of a particular year in an under-graduate course, disqualifies a student to enrol himself in the same class next year. In other words, he loses an opportunity to improve himself just because he failed in the annual examination. Nothing can be more discouraging a system of learning than this. The student is only allowed to sit as a private student for the same class next year. Demoralised thereby, the student loses the sense of right and wrong in his mission to get through the exam as a private student for, he has to obtain a degree at any cost eventually. The unlawful means syndrome creeps into the mind at this juncture. *After all why should an examination deprive an opportunity of learning ?* This needs to be addressed in all sincerity, if the examinations have to be of any meaningful purpose.

Performance Parameters: Toppers versus Paupers

It is often experienced that an examination has marks as a means for rating the performance of a student. One who gets the highest number of marks is regarded as the topper and the one who gets the least is but a pauper. This is a very obnoxious system of evaluating the performance of a student. Knowledge is always relative and contextual. Setting parameters to assess the performance by way of marks is not a judicious method of evaluating an individual. Just as in sports or in matches winning and losing is a matter of timing and preparedness; in academics too, securing the highest number of marks is just a matter of opportunity, preparedness and once social, educational, or even economic background. Students coming from different streams of society cannot be treated as equal in an examination, no matter how much training was imparted. In place of pyramidical structure of evaluation, we can adopt an hexagonal or a pentagonal structure for grading the students through grades in place of marks. This is the practice in most of the advanced countries of the world. Clustering students in grades through their performance is more scientific and justifiable as there is an element of encouragement to all. It is high time that in India, we adopt this system of grading in all institutions. However, it is heartening to know that all the central universities have introduced this system of evaluation years ago.

Awarding of marks on tests or performances based on subjective nature such as practicals in science subjects or field work in various other courses must undergo a drastic change towards better. Favouritism, bias lead to subjective assessment of students bringing blemish on the system of examination. Evaluation of this sort of performance need to be more democratically structured by constitution of committees with teachers to ensure fair play and transparency. Every assessment of performance must have a tangible proof or a well documented record to be available for everybody' perusal. Or else, the examinations would lose the very sanctity that they are characterized with.

Learning and Evaluation – A Continuous Process

There has been a prolonged debate with regard to implementation of semester system in government colleges at under graduate level. In the traditional system of teaching and evaluation, annual examinations were the only climax of completion of a particular course for a particular year. Now, in all the central universities and in most of the other universities, semester plan has been implemented wherein examinations are conducted for each semester and the marks of evaluation are added in the end to arrive at the aggregate percentage or grade of a particular student. This method of examination is in my opinion the best scheme, for it assesses the content learnt by the student in regular intervals. Besides, the student has an opportunity to improve himself after each semester with an aim to prove himself eventually. The examinations in a semester system are less taxing and more encouraging because the content for which the examination is held is limited and the student having number of semesters in a course feels secure for, he can always make up for his lesser performance in one semester with better performance in another.

Unlike in the annual examination system where a student is burdened with insurmountable task of memorizing, recollecting, storing in mind various topics only to pour out at the end of the year, in a semester system, the mind of the student is relatively relaxed, as he keeps clearing the stock of stored material in the mind at regular intervals while at the same time learning new things. Similarly, the content of the examination also keeps changing from semester to semester making it easier for examiners to concentrate on paper setting with relatively higher quality and focus. Thus semester system has a lot to contribute towards continuous process of learning and examining, which is ideal for a true pedagogic scheme.

Participation of Students as a Part of Examination

As we discussed in the earlier pages, teaching need not necessarily be one sided. It is a two-way process of exchanging notes between the students and the teachers. Besides written examinations, a certain percentage of evaluation must in all cases be reserved for assessing the personality development of a student in terms of skills of communication, analysis and presentation. This sort of an exercise is normally seen in law courses wherein the students compulsorily participate in mock trials and arguments known as 'mute courts'. The same can be replicated in Humanities and Sciences as well. This helps students to remember better, whatever they have learnt in the classroom and present it in a cogent and cohesive manner. The result of such a classroom participation will bridge the gap between the teachers and the taught. The marks awarded to each student on the basis of the participation of student can be added to the aggregate at the end of the year. A system of such an evaluation makes learning and evaluation a pleasant pursuit.

Paper setting

Paper setting in other words known as preparing a question paper in an examination is the most important part of evaluation and assessment of a student's knowledge. It is a common story in most of the institutions that same questions keep repeating year after year, which makes it convenient for students to avoid extensive preparation for examinations. The market gets swarmed up by keys, guides, 20 question books etc., making things worse. For a meaningful examination, a loud thinking needs to go into the concept of paper setting. Questions asked must be based on analytical requirements as a necessary component of answer. Only in such an event, a student feels the necessity to read the subject matter in detail and in totality. Answers given by students to such questions would reflect their ability to put forth their thoughts with required connectivity of concepts and proper understanding of the intricacies involved in. After all, the aim of an examination is not necessarily to fail or pass a student. Rather it is a means to evaluate his knowledge and assess his grooming as an educated citizen. It will also be prudent to seek intervention from the student community with regard to question paper setting and collect mock questions from them in order to give due importance to their feelings in the question paper. This is a true participatory approach towards learning.

Conclusion

Examination reforms is a vast and vexing subject that it is practically difficult to arrive at straight jacket suggestions without regard to time and space. However, I feel that written examinations have their unquestionable importance as they are factual documents for a student's performance. Besides written examination is the best form of eliminating the personal bias subjectivity as, the answer sheets are evaluated with coded secrecy and with complete transparency. Examination needs to be a more pleasant form of assessment than a nightmare to the students. The fear syndrome associated with examinations needs to be eliminated from the entire process. This is only possible giving a long rope to a student to prove him or herself over a period of time through semester system. Participation of students in the learning process makes it easier for them to face the examinations with ease, comfort and confidence.

The procedures associated with examination needs to be less cumbersome and more student friendly. Insistence on rigid formalities takes away the spirit of assessment and evaluation which is the underlying theme of an examination.

Trust and respect towards students as dignified human beings is an essential requirement in an examination hall situation. Examinations are not meant to be a trap to nab the delinquent elements who resort to unlawful means. The basic cause for such a trend towards unlawful means needs to be investigated than devising more and more techniques to arrest the same. *We should remember that symptoms must not be mistaken for disease. The malady is the lacklustre performance of institutions in terms of pedagogic instruction and personality development of students.* The young minds have to be attracted towards learning in the most inspiring ways possible in place of traditional dogma- '*Spare the rod and spoil the child*'.

To sum up, reforms in the examination have to be based on the need to improve the knowledge of a student and to orient him towards higher learning. The academic fraternity should realize that imparting knowledge and assessing a student is not a one way system of communication. On the other hand, it is symbiotic relationship between the two. It is ironical that even with so-called stringent methods of examinations, we are only generating degrees which fetch no life chances or job opportunities for students in this modern world. Elimination is the aim of competitive examinations for recruitments as thousands and lakhs sit for the same to qualify for a job. In an academic environment, such an intent (elimination) is uncalled for, for the simple reason that passing or failing in an annual examination is not going to make a difference in the immediate run. The object of the examination is to ensure learning by a student rather than insisting on victory at the 'finish' as it happens in sports. It is time that a serious thought has gone into the entire schema of things.

4

Exemptions to Right to Information

This paper is an attempt to examine the circumstances under which information can be withheld under the Right to Information Act, 2005 by defining the right provisions provided in the said Act and to analyse the decisions of the Central Information Commission under Section 8 of the Right to Information Act, 2005. The project also aims at answering questions as to (a) under which Section/provision can the information asked for, may be withheld, (b) how does the Central Information Commission interpret the Section 8 of the Right to Information Act, 2005. This paper aims, basically, at analysing Section 8 of the Act with the help of cases /appeals, decisions and comments available in the contemporary legal parlance.

The Act on Right to Information, came into force on 12th October 2005 giving to the citizens the right to ask, inquire and disclosure of information from the public authorities. The Act also mentions certain provisions under which the information sought for can be denied. The paper strictly deals with such provisions, confined strictly to Section 8, and the decisions of the established body created under the Act namely the Central Information Commission. The main aim of the paper is to identify the provision which exempts the governmental bodies from the disclosure of information and whether the Commission as mentioned above has been interpreting the provision in the spirit of the Act. The first part of this work deals with brief description of Act, while the second part deals with the provisions relating to exemption from disclosure of information. Finally we analyse various comments on the decisions of the Commission. In the end we sum up in brief the relevance and scope of the subject.

HISTORICAL BACKGROUND AND SCOPE

The history of the Act dates back to the Official Secrets Act of 1889, later amended in the year 1923, enacted during the British rule to protect information related to the security and sovereignty of the country and foreign relations with other states. In the landmark case of Raj Narain vs. State of UP in 1975[1] the Supreme Court held that right to information is a fundamental right under Article 19(1) of the Constitution because if the people do not know or are not aware of the practices of the government or any information whatsoever meant to be known to them then they cannot speak. Hence availability of information is a fundamental right. The Central Government in order to pass a nation wide law on availability of information and eradication of corruption plus allied problems, which the Right to Information Act has achieved on a massive scale, appointed a committee under H.D. Shourie to draft legislation which became the basis of the Freedom of Information Act, 2002 but because of flaws it could never come into effective force. With the failure in enacting the law at that time, the government finally on 15th June 2005 (w.e.f. 12th October 2005) was successful in passing the Right to Information Act.[2] The Act gives right to ask for information from all constitutional authorities or bodies created by an act of Parliament or state legislature. The Act covers entire India except the state of Jammu and Kashmir. It is also applicable to those bodies which are "owned, controlled, or substantially financed"[3] by government or those non-government organizations which are funded either directly or indirectly by the government.

Private bodies are exempted from giving information under this act. However, the information that can be asked or accessed by the government can also be requested for by the citizens[4]. In 2006 the Central Information Commission in the case of Sarbajit Roy vs. DERC[5] held that companies which are privatized but the government owns shares in the company then, it amounts to government body and information asked for, needs to be provided. The Act from the date of its commencement on 13th October 2005 has an overriding effect on the Official Secrets Act and other laws in force till date[6].

Main Features of the Act

The main objective of the Act is to give to the citizens of India, the right to ask for information from any government body to know about the policies, laws, decisions or any other information which affects them or their rights directly or indirectly. Following are the main features of the Right to Information Act, 2005:

- Definitions of various terms under Section 2
- Process through which information can be obtained
- Defining a format for the requisition of information
- The charges for applying for the information
- Time period in which information has to be made available and the penalty, in the form of fine, if the requirement is not met out in time
- Various provisions stating obligation on part of the public authorities under Section 4(1), designation of Public Information Officer under Section 5, request for obtaining information under Section 6, disposal of request under Section 7, restriction on information under Section 8
- Chapter III, IV and V deals with Central and State Information Commission and their powers
- Chapter VI deals with miscellaneous information like protection of action taken in good faith under Section 21, Exempted Organizations like Intelligence

Bureau, Aviation Research Centre, National Security Guards etc. provided in the Second Schedule and under Section 24 of the Right to Information Act[7].

EXEMPTIONS TO THE RIGHT

All said and done the act does not confer an unfettered right to information on any subject or with regard to any individual. Section 8 of the Right to Information Act deals with the circumstances under which information can be withheld. The Act limits citizens from the access of information, held by the government bodies as confidential or in economic or social welfare etc. Section 8(1) lists various provisions under which information can be withheld unless and until the requested information is in public interest and more important and necessary than private interest in the disclosure of information as stated under Section 8(2) of the Act. It is expected on the part of the Public Information Officers to create a clear understanding of the provisions, so that the denial of the requested information does not violate the provisions of Section 8(1) of the Right to Information Act and which might lead to confusion, harassment, delay or any form of physical or mental stress or loss of time or opportunity for the requester of the information or any such thing which might lead to corruption, denial etc. on part of the public authorities.

The Act through its various provisions under Section 8(1) acts as a reasonable restriction by safeguarding information which may lead to national crisis or loose foreign relations with other states, disclosure of information which should not be made available in the public orinformation which might come in the way of individual privacy as held by the Supreme Court in the Neera v. L. I. C. Case[8] in 1992, that demand or disclosure of personal information violates the provision of right to privacy provided in Article 21 of the Indian Constitution. Also, the Act provides in its second schedule under Section 24 the organisations which cannot be approached for information acting again as a circumstance under which information can be withheld[9]. For the purpose of this paper, only provisions under Section 8 will be dealt with.

The following are the provisions under the Section 8(1) through which information can be withheld:

(a) Information which on disclosure would result in negatively affecting the sovereignty and integrity of India or affect the security or economic interests or strategic or scientific aspects of the country also which might lead to the provocation of an offence or which would determine the foreign relations with other countries.

(b) Information forbidden to be disclosed by a court which on disclosure may result in contempt of court.

(c) Information which on disclosure would infringe the privilege of Parliament or State Legislature.

(d) Information which concerns trade or commercial secrets which may harm the competitiveness.

(e) Information available due to a relation of trust between people.

(f) Information received from foreign government with the confidence that the secrecy of the information will be maintained.

(g) Information leading to the identification of the source of information or which may result in life or physical threat of any person.

(h) Information affecting the course of investigation.

(i) Information regarding the records of the decisions taken by the Council of Ministers, Secretaries or other officer.

(j) Information regarding personal information which has no relevance to any public authority and would rather result in infringement of individual privacy.[10]

Following cases dealt by the Central Information Commission will make some of these provisions clear.

With regard to ongoing investigation: (Section 8(1) (g) & 8(1) (h) of the RTI Act)

In the case of Ravinder Kumar Vs. B.S. Bassi, Jt. Commissioner, Police[11], the Central Information Commission dismissed the appeal stating that the disclosure of information in cases which are under investigation by the police was exempted under the provisions of Sections 8(1) (g) and 8(1) (h) of the RTI Act. because disclosure of information may hamper or impede the process of investigation. In the case of R.C. Sankhla, IRS vs. Central Bureau of Investigation, Anti Corruption[12], it was held that the appellant's request for production of certified copies pertaining to his life and liberty was not justified because, the appellant was still on service and was leaving a normal life which meant that there was no immediate threat to his life and liberty. Furthermore, the investigation process on the said file contained information about the appellant's prosecution. Therefore the disclosure of information or permission for the inspection of files at this stage by the appellant would have an impeding effect on the process of prosecution of offender.

Information of fiduciary nature: (Answer scripts of examinations) [Sec. 8(1) (e) of the RTI Act]

In the case of Teresa Irish vs. CPIO, Postal Circle, Trivandrum[13] the appellant, a candidate in a depart-mental examination filed an application for information in the form of a copy of her evaluated answer sheet. The Commission held that there exists a relationship of trust between the authority conducting the examination and the examinee. Section 8(1) (e) provides for fiduciary relationship which exempts the disclosure of information in a fiduciary relationship. Applying the same principle the access to answer scripts in the said case was denied.

Similarly in the case of D.S. Meena vs. CPIO, North Western Railways[14], where the appellant had sought for information seeking for photo copies of answer booklets in the selection of AMM Group 'B', 70% quota North Western Railways held on 9.7.2005, the Central Information Commission held on the basis of the Teresa Irish vs. CPIO, Postal Circle, Trivandrum[15] that the CPIO, North Western Railways was justified in its decision of withholding the information.

Commercial Secrets: (Section 8 (1) (d) and 11(1) of the Act)

In the case of Ramesh Shetty, Impex Statistics Services Vs. The Chief Commissioner of Customs (DZ)[16], Central Information Commission held that the disclosure of the names of the importer/exporter in the daily list has been forbidden by rules as notified by the notification No. 128/2004-Cus (NT) dated 19.11.2004, which further stated to be having the legal force of parliament, thus the exemption from disclosure of information is justified under the Section 8(1) (d) of the Right to Information.

Information Infringing Individual Privacy

In the case of A.P. Singh vs. Punjab National Bank[17], the Central Information Commission held that under Section 8(1) (j) of the RTI Act the bank was justified in refusing to give the information because, the appellant had no relationship with the bank furthermore, the information asked for was not in the concern of public interest rather it was sought for personal interest and the bank is under the duty to maintain secrecy and confidentiality of different accounts. Therefore, the bank's decision was in accordance with the Section 8(1) (j) of the RTI Act.

Income tax returns exempted from disclosure under Section 8(1) (j) (*Reference: Farida Hoosenally vs. The Chief Commissioner of Income Tax-IX; 22/IC (A)/ 2006-30th March 2006*[18])

In the case of Manoj K. Kamra vs. Punjab National Bank, Zonal Office, Jaipur[19 20]. the Commission held that, the details of loan account being personal information and also a matter of commercial secrecy the exemptions under Sections 8(1) (d), (e), (j) apply here and the bank is correct in denying information to the appellant.

Exempted bodies under Section 24

Case: In the case of Shri Sarjeet Singh vs. Directorate General, Central Reserve Police Force (CRPF)[21] the appellant wanted information regarding an advisory memo issued to him by the DIGP, CRPF, Silchar (Assam) on a complaint, while posted in 151 Bn, CRPF. the Central Information Commission held that CRPF was exempted from giving information unless the case of human rights violation or corruption arises. Therefore, the Central Information Commission dismissed the appeal.

CRITIQUE on the Decisions of CIC

The Decisions of Central Information Commission under Section 8 of the Right to Information Act, 2005 have been both liberal and broad, depending on the merits of each case. In some cases the very basic interpretation of the statute has been taken into consideration and in some cases, the Central Information Commission went to wider understanding of the provision and gave landmark decisions under the section 8 of the Right to Information Act. The appeals to the Central Information Commission used in this paper and some other cases will be dealt with to support this proposition.

In **Teresa Irish vs. CPIO, Postal Circle, Trivandrum**[22] The Commission held that the examinee and the authority conducting the exam have a fiduciary relationship.There cannot be any relationship in this situation because, for a relation of trust, there must be recognition of both the parties which lacked here. Therefore, the decision taken by the Commission, though broad, did not qualify to be correct in delivering. Example: doctor and patient. A doctor is bound by his duty to do the best possible and help the patient in any way possible but the same does not apply here However in **George Paul vs. B.S.N.L**[23], the commission again delivered the same decision stating that the examiner and the examinee are in a fiduciary relationship hence, the information cannot be disclosed but in the second part of the decision B.S.N.L. was ordered to disclose the marks of other candidates. This time, the decision has been taken on a wider interpretation of the provision. This is because the disclosure of marks of other candidates will lead to a manipulation free selection process in the case of a competitive-cum-qualifying exam held by the public authority. Thus, the question of 'larger public interest' has been answered.

In **Satyapal vs. CPIO, TCIL**[24] the Commission observing that file notings was an integral part of a file and information cannot be denied, held that the exemption from disclosure as held by the CPIO, TCIL under Section 8(1) (d) and (e) of RTI Act was not justified and every citizen has the right to information on file notings and thus Satyapal should be provided with the requested information. In this case, the decision taken by the Commission was based on a broad construction of Section 8 under the RTI Act, 2005 because instead of working on literal terms the Commission defined various provisions and then finally decided in favour of the appellant.

In **Shri Kamal Anand vs. Central Board of Direct Taxes (CBDT) Ministry of Revenue, Department of Finance**[25] the appellant requested for information regarding the scrutiny policy of the CBDT claiming it to be in the public interest. The appeal was dismissed even after much persuasion and logical forcefulness of the appellant's arguments. This appeal, as per the author, is indeed a case where the Commission took a broad meaning of the Section 8 otherwise a literal meaning would have led the appellant win over the CBDT with his persuasive arguments. In *Sunil Kumar Pathak vs. Central Bank of India, Zonal Office, Raipur*[26] the Commission under Section 8(1) (b) held that the information requested could not be provided since the matter was under judicial examination. The Commission through this decision did literal interpretation of the Section 8.

Conclusion

The above analysis explains the Act and the provisions of section 8 providing for the exemptions under which information can be denied along with comments in the form of analysis, on the decisions taken by the Central Information Commission. It can be concluded that the Act acts as a deterrent on the maladministration prevalent in the government bodies. Furthermore it gives the power to ask for justifications for the decisions taken by the public authority. We can emphatically say that the exemptions as provided are a necessity to safeguard the interest of the state and individuals associated with the sovereign functions of the state. The absence of these provisions may lead to chaos, loss of personal liberty and privacy and endanger the existence of State. Through various judgments, it has been tried to justify the above mentioned proposition that it is not just the Act which limits citizens from getting information through exempted provisions but it is the Central Information Commission too which makes sure that the provisions are interpreted in the spirit of the Act and neither denial or allowance is permitted by misconstruing the exemptions.In short the exemptions are a safety valve of the act.

REFERENCES

1. (1975) 4 SCC 428
2. *See* P.K. DAS, THE RIGHT TO INFORMATION ACT 2005 (Universal Law Publishing Co. reprint 2006)
3. Right to Information Act, 2005 (22 0f 2005)
4. *Ibid.*
5. Appeal No. CIC/WB/A/2006/00011 Dated: 03/1 Application /'06, available at http://cic.gov.in/CIC_Decisions.htm
6. *Supra note* 3
7. *Supra note* 3
8. AIR 1992 SC 392
9. *Supra note* ;*see also* http://www.pria.org/image/Analysis%20of%20Judgements%20of%20the%20Central%20I nformation %20Commission%20on%20RTI%20Act%202005.pdf
10. *Supra note* 3
11. F. No. CIC/AT/A/2006/00004 Dated 30/6/2006, available at http://cic.gov.in/CIC_Decisions.htm
12. Appeal No. 04/IC(A)/CIC/2006 Dated 03/03/ 2006, available at http://cic.gov.in/CIC_Decisions.htm
13. Appeal No. ICPB/A-2/CIC/2006 Dated 6/2/2006, available at http://cic.gov.in/CIC_Decisions.htm
14. Appeal No. ICPB/A-3/CIC/2006 Dated 10/02/ 2006, available at http://cic.gov.in/CIC_Decisions.htm
15. *Supra note* 13
16. Appeal No. CIC/MA/A/2006/00012 Dated 10/03/2006, available at http://cic.gov.in/CIC_Decisions.htm
17. Appeal No.12/IC (A)/2006 Dated 14/3/2006, available at http://cic.gov.in/CIC_Decisions.htm
18. Appeal No. 22/IC (A)/ 2006 Dated 30/03/2006, available at http://cic.gov.in/CIC_Decisions.htm
19. Appeal No. 17/IC (A)/2006F.No. 11/54/2006-CIC Dated 28/03/2006 available at http://cic.gov.in/CIC_Decisions.htm
20. *Ibid*
21. Appeal No. CIC/WB/A/2007/00458 Dated 02/04/2007, available at http://cic.gov.in/CIC_Decisions.htm

22. *Supra note* 13
23. Appeal No.38/ICPB/2006 Dated 29/6/2006, available at http://cic.gov.in/CIC_Decisions.htm
24. Appeal No.ICPB/A-1/CIC/2006 Dated 06/03/2008, available at http://cic.gov.in/CIC_Decisions.htm
25. Appeal No.CIC/AT/A/2007/00617 Dated 11/02/2008, available at http://cic.gov.in/CIC_Decisions.htm
26. Appeal No.11/IC(A)/2006F.No.CIC/MA/A/2005/00001 Dated 14/03/2006, available at http://cic.gov.in/CIC_Decisions.htm

5

Constitutional Provisions for Affirmative Action : A Review

Introduction

Recently a Movie named 'AARAKHSAN' was banned from screening in some North Indian States for apprehension of Caste based violence. The issue of Mandal Commission's Recommendations and reservations for Backward Classes once again seemed to surface at the national levels. A few thoughts ran across my mind on the policy of social justice in India especially in relation to Class versus Caste controversy.

Human society in the entire world right from the dawn of civilization on this earth has been associated with inequality, oppression and exploitation of fellow human beings in one form or the other. For centuries, majority of human beings have been subjected to ill-treatment, humiliation and oppression be it in the name of race, colour, religion or sex. The Blacks in Africa, the Jews in Europe, the slaves in Rome were some of the examples. The worst ever form of inhuman society can be found unfortunately in the Indian sub-continent for the birth in a particular part of a society happened to be the reason for discriminating human beings irrespective of virtues, character, or talent.

Social justice is the hall mark of a modern and civilized society in sharp contrast with the exploitative social systems of ancient and medieval societies. Equality, equal opportunity in society, justice and absence of discrimination are the chief characteristics of the concept of social justice. The preamble of the constitution of India reflects the heart and soul of the Indian republic with the phrases,

> '....*Resolved to constitute India in to a Sovereign, Socialist, Secular, Democratic, Republic and secure to all it's citizens:*
>
> *Justice, social, economic and political*
>
> *Liberty* of thought, expression, belief, faith and worship
>
> *Equality* of status and opportunity............'

Probably only a few written constitutions in the world may have such commitment to social justice as India does. The commitment is predominant as is seen in majority of provisions of the constitution especially spelt out in Chapter III and IV (the Fundamental Rights and Directive Principles). This commitment is a result of prolonged struggle by the under-privileged and downtrodden sections of people against oppressive and exploitative social order of the country. It is indeed pleasantly surprising that the constitution of India which is enacted for the governance of the state and society does not even mention about caste or caste based hierarchy which has been the bedrock of Indian social order for ages. The credit, undoubtedly, goes to the framers of the Constitution lead by Dr. Ambedkar a great visionary. Besides, abolishing discrimination based on caste, religion or birth, the constitution also makes special provisions through Article 15(4) and 16(4) for the advancement of backward classes and for empowering them by way of making reservations in services under government. There can be no more magnificent example than this to vouch for the commitment of the constitution towards social justice for all the citizens of India.

The intentions of the legislature in framing the constitution though lofty and laudable, a question remains to be answered as to the very relevance of the provisions of social justice in view of ever increasing Caste polarisation and consequent threat to nation as an entity. Whether the constitution could successfully address the issue of social justice in the country is a vexed issue, often appears in almost all forums of debates, discussions and judicial deliberations. In order to understand the issue, we need to dwelve upon the inherent contradictions in the society, in sufficient detail as the basic problems of backwardness, inequality, and exploitation certainly stem from the roots of Indian social structure unlike in any other country. Let us briefly investigate in to the causes that hamper social justice and find out how best they can be addressed.

Caste Antithetic to Equality and Social Justice

Social justice in India has a direct bearing on the caste system as the denial of social justice was only a result of caste hierarchy. Any action by State to ensure social justice has to begin by addressing caste based inequalities. Therefore it would be futile to discuss social justice in isolation.

Caste - a synonym of Indian society, is the only and the most dominant factor that rules the lives of all people. People born in a particular caste are supposed to marry within the same caste and have loyalty, allegiance to their caste without ever thinking of transgressing the barriers of the same. It could have been the happiest thing ever had there been only one caste in India. Unfortunately, there are thousands of castes and thousands of sub-castes each of it having a characteristic and origin. Louis Dumont, French sociologist, gives a vivid picture of this in his magnum opus *Homo Hierarchicus*. The Jajmani system in ancient India, according to Dumont, gave birth to stratification of the society, based on occupational diversity guided by the principles of division of labour. More than stratification, the caste in India is a hierarchical form of human groups with strict distinction of superior and inferior status.

Manu, the ancient law giver of Hindu religion clearly spells out 4 castes or Varnas known as Brahmin, Kshatriya, Vaishya and Shudra. The first 3 are categorized as twice borne (who perform the sacred thread ceremony), whereas the fourth category the Shudras are once born and are supposed to be indulged in servitude for the benefit of the first 3 Varnas. The following verses of *Manusmriti* reveal the unscientific and exploitative nature of Indian society that is characterized by caste or varna.

Manu (*in Chapter 1 verse 31*) says:-

"But for the sake of the prosperity of the worlds He (God) caused the Brahmin, the Kshtriya, the Vaisya and the Shudras (the four Castes) to proceed from his mouth, his arms, his thighs and his feet.

In other verses, as following, the inequalities of Hindu Caste hierarchy are prominent.

96. A man of low caste who through covetousness lives by the occupations of a higher one, the king shall deprive of his property and banish.

121. If a Shudra, unable to subsist by serving Brahmins seeks a livelihood, he may serve Kshatriya, or he may also seek to maintain him by attending on a wealthy Vaisya.

128. The more a Shudra, keeping himself free from envy, imitates the behavior of the virtuous, the more he gains, without being censured, exaltation in this world and the next.

The caste system in India is marked by glaring inequalities and exploitation of the inferior Varna or caste. Caste is peculiar to Hindu society. Nevertheless, the minorities such the Muslims and Christians though profess different religion from Hindu also have caste as a additional identification. This is primarily because of conversions. The adverse impact of Indian caste system is evident in the social, political and economic fields Majority of millions of people suffering from hunger, disease, happened to belong to the down-trodden castes which are otherwise known as the lower castes. Denial of equality, equal opportunity for centuries to these people is a historical fact. It is on the advent of British in India, the modern concepts of liberalism, secularism, and rationality found way into Indian society

Socialistic Republic with no Social Justice

The Constitution though declares India a socialistic republic we fail to find any constitutional arrangement to this end barring Directive Principle of Chapter IV which are more a list of commandments for charity than Rights. The economy and the polity has always been dominated by handful of castes known as the higher castes while the majority of other castes were assigned the jobs of servitude. Here it is contextual to quote V.P. Singh the then Prime Minister and chief architect of OBC reservations. In his speech in parliament Mr. Singh said:

> *'What is the merit of the system itself? That the section which has 52% of the population gets 12.55% in Government employment. What is the merit of the system? That is Class I employees of the Government it gets only 4.69%, for 52% of the population; in decision-making at the top echelons it is not even one-tenth of the population of the country; in the power structure it is hardly 4.69%. I want to challenge first the merit of the system itself before we come and question on the merit, whether on merit to reject this individual or that. And we want to change the structure basically, consciously, with open eyes.'*[1]

The Weaker sections still toil in brick kilns, municipal drains, construction sites while spending nights in make shift houses and slums at the out skirts of cities and towns. Every year the rural migration to cities in search livelihood (and social respect too) is on the rise. Majority of this lot is from weaker sections. What relevance does the concept of socialist republic have when it could not bring about any change in the traditional mode of production that denied equality of opportunity. What is required today is a wholesale social engineering aimed at social justice to all irrespective of caste or class. We need to learn from our mistakes and make renewed efforts towards achieving an egalitarian human society in place of a caste society.

Provisions for Social Justice

No wonder, concern for social justice in favour of those castes who were exploited by the Indian social order became natural for the State. The govt. of India Act 1935 brought the term "Scheduled Castes" into use, and defined the group as including "such castes, races or tribes or parts of groups within castes, races or tribes, which appear to His Majesty in Council to correspond to the classes of persons formerly known as the 'Depressed Classes', as His Majesty in Council may prefer." After independence, the Constituent Assembly continued the prevailing definition of Scheduled Castes and Scheduled Tribes, and gave (via articles 341, 342) the President of India and Governors of states responsibility to compile a full listing of castes and tribes, and also the power to edit it later as required. The actual complete listing of castes[2] and tribes was made via two orders respectively[3]. Backward Classes was the genre which includes Scheduled Castes and Scheduled Tribes besides other castes known as OBC (Mandal Commission's recommendations). The Non-Dalit /Tribe sections and castes were later included for protective discrimination with a view to ensure social justice.

The most important concern of the Constituent Assembly happened to be the abolition of caste-based discrimination in the country, besides imparting justice to the historically discriminated and exploited sections of citizens. This has led to two important provisions in the Constitution. They are article 15(4) and 16(4). These two provisions have opened the doors of development and empowerment for the hitherto neglected and oppressed citizens known as, Scheduled Castes Scheduled Tribes and Backward Classes.

Some relevant clauses of Article 15 and Article 16 are as under:

Art. 15. says;

(1) The State shall not discriminate against any citizen on grounds only of religion, race, caste, sex, place of birth or any of them.

(4) Nothing in this article or in clause (2) of Article 29 shall prevent from making any special provision for the advancement of any socially and educationally backward classes of citizens or for the Scheduled Casts and Scheduled Tribes.'

Art. 16 says;

(1) There shall be equality of opportunity for all citizens in matters relating to employment or appointment to any office under the State.

(2) No citizen shall, on grounds only of religion, race, caste, sex, descent, place of birth, residence or any of them, be ineligible for, or discriminated against in respect of, any employment or office under the State.

(4) Nothing in this Art shall prevent the State from making any provision for the reservation of appointments or posts in favour of any backward class of citizens which, in the opinion of the state, is not adequately represented in the services under the State.

(Clause (4a) inserted by the Constitution (77th Amendment) Act, 1995, w.e.f. 17-6-1995.)

It is significant to note, that Art. 15 & 16 have not defined what a backward class is or what a Scheduled Caste and Scheduled Tribe is. Dr. Amedkar expressed that "*a backward community is a community that is backward in the opinion of the Government*"[4] The underlying theme in the above two fundamental rights with their exceptions as discussed above is not only to ensure equality before law and equal protection of law but also to provide special opportunities for those classes of citizens to be equal to obtain the benefits of these two fundamental rights in comparison with the relatively better off citizens of the country who do not suffer from the backwardness as visualized by Art. 15(4).

Supreme Court and Interpretation of Art. 15 and 16

The Supreme Court had laid down clear and path finding principles of law by way of interpreting Articles 15 and 16 in a number of cases, with regard to scope of 15(4) and effect of 16(4) in relation to 16(1). It was held that preferential treatment of backward class and Scheduled Caste and Scheduled Tribes is a rational classification and is indeed necessary to make effective the equality of opportunity for all citizens which is provided by Art. 16(1)[5]. Clause (4) is an exception to Cl. (1)[6] in so far as it forbids discrimination on the ground of 'race' or 'caste'. It is also in the nature of an exception to Art. 29(2) [7]

Caution was exercised by Supreme Court saying that however Cl. (4) cannot be so extended as in effect to destroy the guarantee in Cl(1.).[8] Unless the test of backwardness is objectively satisfied mere good faith of the authorities cannot protect a discriminatory provision under Cl. (4).[9] Element of subjectivity has no place in this regard. The special provisions permissible under Art. 15(4) are not just confined to positive action programmes alone for the advancement of backward classes but would also include 'reservation' in educational institutions and other walks of life[10] Art. 15(4) envisages the policy of compensatory or protective discrimination but it should be reasonable and consistent with ultimate public interest i.e. national interest and the interest of community or society as a whole.[11] Above all the Right to Equality remains undisputed.

Clause (4) of article 15 is a general provision made for the advancement of backward classes including scheduled castes and tribes as an exception to the clause (1) because apparently it goes against the spirit of equality. Going a bit further the constitution in sub-clause (4) of article 16 emphatically makes provision for empowerment of backward classes by way of reservation of jobs in government services. This sub-clause also includes scheduled castes and tribes for they too are backward classes. Broadly speaking these two provisions are meant for imparting social justice for the backward classes which in other words and in practical terms known as, SC, ST and other backward classes (castes).

The Court was firm in ruling that Article 15(4) is an enabling provision, like Art. 16(4), and the reservation, under either provision, should not exceed legitimate limits.[12] It does not create any fundamental right in favour of a member of the classes specified in Art. 14.[13]

The object of (the 1st) Amendment was to bring Arts. 15 and 29 in line with Art. 16(4)[14]." However, Art. 16(4) refers to "backward class of citizens", whereas Art. 15(4) refer to "socially and educationally backward class of citizens or for Schedule Castes and Schedule Tribes." The difference between Art. 15(4) and Art. 16(4) is striking, but, as will appear hereafter, the words "backward classes" have been judicially interpreted as covering the same classes as are referred to in Art. 15(4). Permissible classification for affirmative action must satisfy two conditions, namely, (1) it must be founded on an intelligible differentia which distinguishes persons or things that are grouped together from others left out of the group, and (ii) the differentia must have a rational relation to the object sought to be achieved by the statute in question.[15]

Reservations and Social Justice : Two Sides of the Same Coin

It is to compensate for the discrimination perpetrated against certain communities in the name of caste for centuries in the country. It is positive discrimination towards some classes of citizens aimed at imparting social justice to them. Today, reservations are common in almost all educational institutions and in public recruitments. The recommendations of Mandal Commission for a provision of 27% reservations for other backward classes has been historic and epoch making event in the post-independent India. Now besides SC and ST certain other castes categorized broadly as backward classes are also roped in with a view to empower them with the principle of social justice underneath. Principle of adequate representation (Art.16(4) happened to be the governing factor behind recommendations for reservations in favour of the backward classes. All the provisions of reservations have been constitutionally guaranteed through various constitutional amendments.

The essence that emanates from the above actions of State is simple i.e. ensuring social justice to the historically downtrodden and exploited classes of people who are categorized as lower castes and Dalits in Hindu social set-up. Surely, the intention of the legislature and the content of the constitution is noble and praiseworthy.

But however the question remains to be answered is whether the intentions of the constitution have been really translated into action in meeting the avowed goals of social justice.

The Immortal Caste Syndrome

Caste consciousness and demand for inclusion is glaringly present in the post independent India having its all pervading influence and impact on the polity and economy of the country. Though the constitution intended to show a justifiable bias in favour of the depressed and exploited classes/castes, it seems, alongside, it has generated serious side effects in terms of polarization of castes and politicization of electoral process. The irony is, no matter whether the backward classes could enjoy the benefit of social justice or not, the historically dominant castes have become conscious of their existence and left no stone unturned in securing the same by consolidating their strength in terms of economy and politics. It is a fact even today that the candidates from scheduled castes and scheduled tribes cannot ensure their electoral success in the event of their contesting from an unreserved constituency. This scenario is less intense in case of candidates belonging to backward castes. The majority being the backward castes amounting to around 57%, to borrow Mandal's propositions, they could ensure their relatively better position in politics in the country by dint of their numerical strength. Political leaders from backward castes have been making their mark in Indian politics even with out reserved constituencies.

On the other hand, the upper castes have their domination in the society more or less intact, be it in politics or be it in economic development. It is interesting to note that though caste based hierarchy or domination has been abolished in the constitution, the upper castes still continue to hold on to their relatively better position. In other words the provisions of social justice, equality in the constitution appear to have been reduced to nullity as the society at large seems to accept the domination of the upper castes by one way or the other. The democratic process of India too seems to have acknowledged their domination through ballot. Here lies the crux of the problem. What went wrong the masterpiece of the document called the Indian Constitution? If we conduct a survey as to the social background of all the members of the parliament, we will not be disappointed in testing our hypothesis that almost all of them barring the reserved candidates reach parliament purely on the basis of their age-old superior position of their caste, influence and domination associated with it. To borrow the phrase of Tom Bottomore, the sociologist, we may call these castes as the *elites* of Indian *society*. These are *'dominant castes'* to quote M.N. Srinivas-renowned sociologist of India

Defective Strategies and Misplaced Priorities

The caste based reservations though aimed at imparting social justice have brought along with them unwanted problems which begin to threaten the unity, integrity and secular fabric of the nation. This is largely due to ill conceived strategies and hasty priorities that influenced the respective legislations which we can describe as under.

'Not Adequately Represented' : A Phrase Ignored

The protective discrimination as laid down in article 15(4) is aimed at making special provisions for the advancement of SC, ST and OBC with regard to many fields such as economic, educational or social. But it does not provide for reservations in government services. The position is different in so far as the article 16 (4) is concerned where by it was exclusively spelt out that appointments can be made in government employment for those *'not adequately represented'*. It is important to note here that the State in India has taken quick interest in article 16(4) by affirmative action through reservations in jobs. It appears that the State is of the view that by provision of few jobs in favour of weaker sections, it is going to ensure their social and educational advancement on par with the forward classes (castes) of the society. The provision along with the phrase of 'not adequately represented' appears to be impractical condition. Because, firstly backward class was never defined by the constitution and secondly there was no legislation to such an effect so as to maintain a caste-wise data of representation in government services across the country. Thirdly there no adequate number of jobs in the country to be given to the *Not adequately represented.* Job reservations seem to be more a lolly pop given to a few while millions of weaker sections struggle as labourers. However it is not to deny the representative aspect of the provision so far as the empowerment of weaker section is concerned. Never the less it is also a fact that the target group is divided in to *Haves* and *Have nots* as there are no adequate number of jobs for all. Here the *survival of fittest* (Herbert Spencer) among the weaker sections matters. The *Cream* survives the test and transforms in to a self recruiting elite. So can we assure social justice to all? It is a serious issue needs to be addressed with equal seriousness.

Art. 16(4) vs Art. 15(4) :Putting the Cart before the Horse

It is intriguing as to why the State had to take recourse to Art.16 (4), a discretionary provision, making it mandatory while Atr.15(4) in self has enough to provide in support of classified legislation. Art.15 (4) is a precursor to Art.16(4) and the latter is complimentary to the former. In such a situation, it is but natural to arrive at a conclusion that, the state is putting the cart before the horse, because despite making a provision of reservation of jobs according article 16(4), it is not guaranteed practically that the classified class of citizens would take advantage of the same. For the simple reason that, reservation does not mean direct appointment on the posts. The stakeholders are supposed to sit for an examination for recruitment which is compulsory. It is important to realize here that within the stakeholders there happens to be competition. This is where the early birds catch the worms; in other words, the competent stakeholders naturally get selected for recruitment and the less competent are left-out. *Here it is significant that there works equally the yardstick of merit even among the backwards. Therefore, the competition is among the in-equals within the classified group.*

The situation calls for an intervention on the part of the state to regulate the affirmation action. In other words, the backward linkages such as adequate educational infrastructure sufficient number of seats in academic institutions, special training classes for competitive exams, hostel facilities for students, proper income generating schemes for the parents of the stakeholders etc. are very much required in order to provide equality of opportunity in true sense of the term to ensure a reasonable, though not, proportional representation from at least majority of the castes within the *special class*. In the absence of such a pro-active programme or pre-emptive initiative on the part of the state, the advantage of article 16(4) would be taken away only by the dominant castes within the so-called special class of citizens which the classified legislation never intended. After all the Art. 16(4) clearly qualified for *'not adequately represented'*. Creation of infrastructure for the economic development of castes is a precondition or else the less advanced can not avail of the quota for employment as they are not even qualified towards that end.

Justice Denied from with in

Whether it is by the affirmative action or protective discrimination, when the State encourages a special class of citizens to join the main-stream by making special provisions, the state has also the responsibility to see to it that these provisions are objective and transparent enough to give effect to the intention of Legislature. But *when a few castes in the special class of citizens keep reaping the fruits of such a legislation, and majority are left behind, then it no longer means a classified legislation. On the contrary, it is a class legislation which the constitution never intended it to be.* For instance_the concept of creamy layer was rendered meaningless as vested interests among the special class of citizens (Backward Classes/castes) have taken advantage of it either by hook or by crook. *The equal protection of law means the equality of people before law who are similarly situated. Here, it seems that within the Backward Classes as a special class of citizens, the concept of equality before law, and the concept of equal protection of law seems to be rendered ineffective as the equally placed categories and castes are not equally encouraged (though treated so) to receive the benefits.* How ever there seems to be shift in the policy by quite a few States as we learn that reservation with in reservation is being made in favour of the most backward of the backward. Still it is too early to reach a positive conclusion.

Class versus Caste

The constitution is secular and does not recognize or encourage any caste in particular, the mention of scheduled castes and tribes in different Articles not-withstanding. It is social and educational backwardness which is taken as reference point for an affirmative action. Article 15(4) specially mentions *"socially and educationally backward classes"*. It is crystal clear that it is a concept of class, which is the qualifying factor for a positive discrimination in one's favour. *Caste as such, has never been recognized in the constitution as a point of identification for educational or social backwardness. However, it is a different matter that in the Indian society which is completely divided on caste lines, caste becomes a sine-qua-non factor for such identification, unwillingly though.* Caste is so important a factor that the polity and democracy of India, it seems, has to live with it. Hence, the concept of social engineering which is the generic philosophy behind the protective discrimination. Nevertheless, constitution of India has not laid emphasis on caste factor when a reference was made to social and economic backwardness. *It is unfortunate and paradoxical that the so-called social engineering which is meant for reforming the society fighting against tradition for the sake of modernity, has to start the process from the base-line of caste identity.*

The Supreme Court laid down principles to identify backwardness. Social backwardness is, in the ultimate analysis, the result of poverty.[16] and as so is likely to be aggravated by considerations of caste but the classification of backwardness cannot be made solely on the basis of caste,[17]; and there may be communities which may be backward in a particular State, such as the Muslims or the Christians, even though they may not recognize castes. Similarly, the occupation[18] or habitation[19] of classes of persons (e.g., people residing in rural areas are generally more backward than those in urban areas) may also contribute to the backwardness.

The criteria of economic backwardness is equally important though it has an inverse relationship with social backwardness. Because, all 'classes' in India are 'castes', but all 'castes' are not classes. In other words, the classes connected with the mode of production of the economy in the traditional India are also known as 'castes' and the backward castes have a direct relationship with the mode of production. However, the upper castes, which had enjoyed higher ritual status (and still do), were actually not the part of the economy – at least some of them. For instance, Kshatriyas and Brahmins have never been associated with the activities of mode of production, typical of any economy. Therefore, it is difficult to over-simplify the concept of 'class' and equate it with 'caste'. However, it need not religiously follow caste criteria at all times. Various judgements of Supreme Court laid emphasis on income to be a part of the criteria. With the change of times, and with the advancement of the society, especially in the 20th century, many castes which were not otherwise classes, have lost their sources of economic sustenance and were subjected to the vagaries of the competitive capitalistic market. As a result, these castes are now economically backward and rather pauperized in many pockets of the country; their ritualistic and social esteem not endangered though. Therefore criteria of economic backwardness cannot and, as a matter of fact, need not be ignored, as it is not antithetic to the concept of social justice. On the contrary it will bridge the gap of ritualistic inequalities between castes for *hunger* is as strong a binding factor as it is divisive.

Traditionalizing Modernity and *vicious circle* of Backwardness

Modernization is defined in terms of secularism and rationality. The Tradition (of India) which harboured inequalities by way of sectarian and communal identities, was supposed to give way to Modernity in due course of time. Nevertheless, the irony is, today with excessive adherence to caste criteria, the tradition seems to be sneaking back into modernity through the back door. Through out the country, we witness an increasing demand for more inclusion of castes associated with caste-related political activities holding the State for ransom. *Tradition needs to be modernized; but on the contrary, in India modernity seems to be getting traditionalised.*

Another appalling feature our social engineering is creation of a pool of backwardness. With some classes (castes) given reservation today, the others naturally over years or decades become backeward. A class rendered backward so, may have to be treated as a special class of citizen after some time in future and need to be given the same protective discrimination to come back into main stream. It kicks off a chain reaction in the society. It will be an endless process of encouraging and discouraging different classes of citizens at different points of time in future creating a *vicious circle* of backwardness.

Unqualified Eternal Protection: A threat to Nationalism

The system of reservation in the name of Caste does not seem to have a qualification of time. If the scheme is for eternity, which it seems at least for now, all the intentions of the constitution aimed at a classless egalitarian, socialistic, and secular society will turn void. The protective discrimination must have a qualification of time and quantity. Or else *sooner or later the citizens of the country will loose the identity as Indians as they prefer to choose the identity of their caste or sub-caste which is immediately beneficial to them than the broader and non-paying identity of 'Indian'.* It is relevant to quote Dr. Ambedkar;

> *"..they (the honorable Members) will find that the view of those who believe and hold that there shall be equality of opportunity, has been embodied in sub-clause (1) of Article 10. It is a generic principle. At the same time,...we had to reconcile this formula with the demand*

made by certain communities that the administration which has now – for historical reasons – been controlled by one community or a few communities, that situation should disappear and that the others also must have an opportunity of getting into the public services. Supposing... We were to concede in full the demand of those communities who have not been so far employed in the public services to the fullest extent, what would really happen is, we shall be completely destroying the first proposition upon which we are all agreed. Namely, that there shall be an equality of opportunity. Therefore the seats to be reserved, if the reservation is to be consistent with sub-clause (1) of Article 10, must be confined to a minority of seats. It is then only that the first principle could find its place in the Constitution and effective in operation... I am sure (the honorable Members) will agree that unless you use come such qualifying phrase. As 'backward' the exception made in favour of reservation will ultimately eat up the rule altogether. Nothing of the rule will remain. That I think,...is the justification why the Drafting Committee undertook...the responsibility of introducing the word 'backward' which, I admit, did not originally find a place in the fundamental right in the way in which it was passed by this Assembly.[20]

Conclusion

Social justice is sine-qua-non for a democratic system of governance as opposed to laissez-a-faire where survival of the fittest is the rule. Modern society has a responsibility to ensure social justice to all its citizens those who happen to be out of the main stream of growth and development.

Paradigm Shift: A Necessity

There needs to be a paradigm shift in the approach to protective discrimination. A true *classified legislation has to be based on the concept of Class and not Caste.* Economic classification is all that is required for it is truly secular and includes all castes and communities. Criteria of caste has of course been employed for identification of social and educational backwardness; however, it is high time in the changed socio-political scenario of 21st century, the government had given a serious thought to prefer class as criteria in place of caste. A proper survey of economic backwardness would surely reveal that hitherto included backward classes including the SCs and STs would again be beneficiaries of protective discrimination besides making room for many other classes which are not only just castes. Or else the caste factor recognized by the State would eat up the vital foundations of Indian democracy rendering the constitution absolutely a paradise for caste politics. 'Backwardness a qualifying term' as Ambedkar felt as a yardstick must be redefined in more secular manner.

Dignity of Labour

Many occupations are still associated more with caste based status and social esteem than basic dignity of labour. Craze for officer like or white collared jobs is still dominant in the society. This is partly due to caste identification with the nature of a specific job and partly due to low wages paid against. The State should seriously contemplate on hiking the wage component of such jobs like sanitation workers, sweepers, medical menial staff, peons, etc. *so that the allurement of income on those jobs will have a glorifying effect and gradually the social disrespect going with the job will finally disappear as all would be encouraged to seek them. In such an eventuality even upper castes would not hesitate to take up such jobs.* Commercialisation of occupations will wash away the caste tag of the job. The State need to involve in a loud thinking and act simultaneously.

Wholesale Social Engineering a must –not Piecemeal

What is required is a wholesale social engineering aimed at removing inequalities of opportunities based on birth, caste or religion. Constitution will remain a piece of antiquity in the absence of strong political will to enact provisions meant for social justice. Inequalities discrimination and exploitation resulting from thousands of years of diabolical and inhuman social order of India cannot be put to an end in 60 years of democratic rule which often polluted by the traditionally dominant factors.

The modernity which signifies rationality and secularism is overpowered by the tradition and interestingly on the contrary it is getting traditionalized. Radical steps are needed to deal with the menace of caste and caste-based social inequalities. The constitution needs to be amended to provide more teeth to the state to address the issue of social justice. Piecemeal social engineering such as few government jobs, few scholarships or few hostels, few houses to rural poor etc. cannot bring about lasting changes towards social justice.

It is the mode of production which Dr. Ambedkar has continuously advocated, that needs to be changed to empower all the depressed and Backward classes in the country. The need of the hour is to think of the next generation and not the next election. We need statesmen to emancipate India from the ignoble blemish of social injustice in place of politicians, who make use of sectarian idioms as handy instruments of political power. It is high time we realized that piecemeal social engineering has done more damage than good. It created *Haves and Have-nots* besides encouraging, day by day, more castes to assert in violent form for inclusion. It has become more a struggle for private justice than social justice.

It is not practical to enumerate a list of detailed measures to address the issue in a few line in this article. The concerns expressed in the earlier paragraphs, however, are worth giving a serious thought for an effective mechanism for realization of social justice in India. Let us sum up by quoting Nehru:

'There is a great danger, whether you deal with an individual or group or community, of giving certain props to that community which give it a false sense of strength which does not belong to it, and when they are removed, suddenly make the community weak. A nation ultimately ought to stand on its own feet. So long as it relies on some external prop, it is not strong. It is weak. So these external props, as I might call them, that is reservation of seats and the rest-may possibly be helpful occasionally in the case of backward groups, but they produce a false sense of strength, and ultimately, therefore, they are not so nearly as important as real educational, cultural and economic advance which gives them inner strength to face any difficulty or any opponent.'[21]

REFERENCES

1. (Reservation for Backward Classes, Akalank Publications, New Delhi, info@akalank.com)
2. The Constitution (Scheduled Tribes) Order 1950.
3. The Constitution (Scheduled Castes) Order, 1950.
4. Dr. B.R. Ambedkar at VII CAD 702.
5. Indra Sawhney vs. Union of India, A.I.R. 1993 S.C. 477 (paras 57, 58, 94a, 292, 396, 399-400).
6. Cf. Indra v. Union of India, AIR 1993 SC 477: 1992 Supp. (3) SCC 217—9-Judges; Ajay Kumar Singh v. State of Bihar, (1944) 4 SCC 401 (para 4) : 1994(2) JT 662-Judges; Devdasan T.v. Union of India, AIR 1964 SC 179: 1964(4 SCR 680.
7. CF. Balaji M.R. v. State of Mysore, AIR 1963 SC 649 : 1963 Supp.(1) SCR 439; casebook, pp. 124-25,130.
8. State of A.P. v. SAgear P., (1968) 2 SCJ 778: AIR 19 68 SC 1379: 1968 (3) SCR 595.
9. State of A.P. c. Sagar P., (1968) 2 SCJ 778: AIR1968 SC 1379:1968 (3)SCR 595
10. Cf. Indra v. Union of India, AIR 1993 SC 477: 1992 supp. (3 SCC 217-9 Judges.

11. Ajay Kumar Singh v. State of Bihar, (1994) 4 SCC 401(para 4): 1994(2 JT 662—3 Judges., Preeti Srivastava (Dr) v. state of M.P. (1999)7 SCC 120 (paras 13,15 and 62): AIR 1999 SC 2894.
12. State of A.P. v. Balram U.S.V>, AIR 1972 SC 1375 (1395): (1972) 1 SCC 660; Rajendran C.A. v. Union of India, AIR 1968 SC 507: 1968 (1 SCR 721).
13. Anil v. Dean Govt. Medical College, Nagpur AIR 1985 Bom. 153 (para 6): Partha S.A. v. State of Mysore, AIR 1961 Mys. 220.
14. D.D. Joshi v. Union ('83) A.SC. 420, 425 pp. 296-7.
15. (M.R. Balaji Vs. Mysore (1963) 1 S.C.R. 439, 455, ('63) A.SC. 649, 657.)
16. Balaji M.R.v. State of Mysore, AIR 1963 SC 649(663): 1963 Supp.(1) SCR 439; Jayasree K.S. v. State of Kerala, AIR 1976 SC 2381:(1976)3 SCC 730.
17. Balaji M.R.. v. State of Mysore, AIR 1963 SC 649(663): 1963 Supp. (1) SCR 439; Jayasree K.S. v. State of Kerala, AIR 1976 SC 2381:(1976)3 SCC 730
18. Jayasree K.S. v. State of Kerala, AIR 1976 SC 2381: (1976)3 SCC 730.
19. Periakaruppan A. v. state of T.N., AIR 1971 SC 2302 : (1971) 1SCC 38.
20. *C.A.D.* Vol. 7, pp. 701-02.
21. Nehru. - The First Sixty Years (ed.) Dorothy Norman. Asia Publishing House, (Bombay 1965) p. 400.

6
Legal Literacy and Women Empowerment

It would be surprising to know that even in a country like England which was known as mother of parliaments, women were given voting rights only in the first quarter of the twentieth century. In many countries across the globe, the so called women liberation and equality for women was recognized only in the twentieth century, India being no exception. Women in almost all religions have never been treated on par with men in social, political and economic fields. The modern era of civilization dating back to roughly two hundred years brought with it a concept of liberty, freedom and equality for all human beings. The role of women was emphasized as a necessary and indispensable part of human development. Never the less the battle is not over. Even today, atrocities, exploitation and discrimination against women is common place in all societies and countries, the western world being no exception. Flourishing trend of human trafficking and prostitution across the world is a glaring spectacle that depicts vulnerable status and position of women, even in the twenty first century. Natural outcome of this state of affairs is further degeneration of women's position in society and unabated struggle for equality and justice. So, what is still required to be done in this area of women empowerment, that is still left undone?

Equality and empowerment are two sides of same coin, so far as women liberation is concerned. Empowerment is a wider concept engrossing economic, political and social fields. Literacy and education is acknowledged as sine-qua-non for women empowerment. It is indeed so. However many times it is hard to explain the prevalence of crime against women who are even educated and literate. Among many other things which lead to women empowerment as is emphasized in many government schemes and legislative enactments, legal literacy and legal education has a prominent place. But the pity is, it has not been given required importance at the implementation level.

In the modern world, the laws are democratically made unlike the king made laws. The modern law is based on the widely accepted concepts of equality, justice and liberty and it is equally important to note that the modern laws have impartial enforcement mechanism overseen by an independent judiciary. India stands out as a unique democratic country throwing the beacon light in this respect. However wide spread legal literacy and legal education is still lacking across the length and breadth of the country in the stake holders.

The percentage of women population in India is almost half of that of men. Women in the vulnerable age group of 15 to 45 years happen to be the worst victims of violence, discrimination and exploitation. In the famous case of Gaurav Jain and Union of India, the Hon'ble Supreme Court of India spoke out its heart for the protection of women and their liberation from the red light areas. The inquiry committee appointed for a fact finding in this regard brought out startling facts with regard to the forced prostitution in four metropolitan cities of Mumbai, Delhi, Kolkata and Chennai. The report said that around 75% of women were school dropouts or had no formal education. It is also very interesting that around 25% of women were educated up to plus two and graduation. Undoubtedly it appears that lack of knowledge of law is one of the main reasons for the absence of the spirit to fight back and to stand up to the exploitative forces in the society. Formal education can never be a substitute to legal education for a simple reason that legal education enlightens an individual about his rights and liabilities, the responsibility of the state and society and enables with the knowledge of various avenues for justice. Besides it ensures confidence and courage in the battle against exploitation and discrimination.

Legal Provisions for Protection of Women

Perhaps the Indian law and the legal system is the best in the world in as much as the protection of women is concerned. There are a plethora of statutes which provide for best protection for women in India besides the major Penal Acts. The procedural laws are no less in extending fullest security and safety for the dignity of women. For instance section 160 of Cr.P.C provides for exemption of women to be present in a police station for any investigation. The Prevention of Domestic Violence Act 2006 has many provisions for seeking protection from State against In-Laws and also seek matrimonial home. The examples are illustrative and not exhaustive. However it is a pity that majority of women never make use of these legal provisions for the simple reason that they are not aware of them. Hence there is a need for women centric legal education.

Let us look at the scenario of crime against women in the country in the last decade and understand some important legal provision connected with. It is surprising that despite constitutional guarantees of justice, social, economic and political and assurances of a life of freedom, equality and dignity, sexual abuse and other heinous crime are ravaging the lives of millions of women who remain a prey to predator in the form of husbands, relatives or friends. The life of an average Indian women is still governed by customs, habits, prejudices and unwritten codes of conduct. At times legal complexities combine with social realities and make the life of an average women insecure and miserable.

It is normally seen that the incidence of Rape, Dowry Death, Torture, Molestation and Eve-teasing have been on the rise despite the presence of law and law enforcing machinery. A casual look at the media coverage in no way gives relief from the past. On the contrary the picture is more demoralizing besides horrifying.

The Law and Women

Unemployment and poverty, alcoholism, marital maladjustment, lack of proper moral education, religion and inefficient legal machinery are considered to be some of the factors responsible for crimes against women. Nevertheless the punitive mechanism and the rights of the women to seek redressal and justice ned not fall victim to the above factors. Here lies the importance of legal education for women for it can be the real weapon of empowerment.

An understanding of different legal provisions and their analysis helps assessing the seriousness better. A prosecution for sexual harassment for example under Section 354 Indian Panel Code requires two factors: to be proved:

- that the accused assaulted or used criminal force against a woman.
- that such assault was with an intention or knowledge that it may or is likely to outrage the modesty of the woman.

Indecency or Obscenity against Women

The law relating to obscenity is codified in Sections 292, 293, and 294 of the Indian Penal Code. In spite of these provisions, there is a tendency to represent women indecently in publications, particularly advertisements which have the effect of denigrating the women. A new law Indecent Representation of Women (Prohibition) Act, 1986 was passed to combat this evil, but women continued to be exploited for economic gains. Section 366 Indian Panel Code deals with kidnapping or abducting a women to compel her to marry against her will or in order that she may be seduced to illicit intercourse, or knowing it to be likely that she will be forced or seduced to illicit intercourse. This section also prescribes punishment for any person who abuses his authority to criminally intimidate a woman or induces her to go from any place with an intent that she may be forced or seduced to have illicit intercourse. Sections 366A and 366B deals with the persuasion of minor girls for the aforesaid purpose. Sections 373 and 374 Indian penal code deal with buying and selling of minor girls for purposes of prostitution.

Unlike the general perception of a layman the word prostitution is not confined just to natural sexual intercourse, it includes any act of lewdness or surrender, of the girls chastity for money. The dedication of minors to the temple as Devdasis also amounts to this crime. Section 361 defines kidnapping from lawful guardianships. The taking need not be by force actual or constructive and it is immaterial whether the girl consents or not. There must be a taking of the child out of the possession of the parents, if a child leaves its parents house for a particular purpose with their consent, it cannot be said to be out of their parents.

Sexual Crimes

Section 362 of the Indian Penal Code says wherever by force compels or any deceitful means induces any person to go from any place is said to abduct that person. The intention of the accused is the basis of the charge. The violation, the intention and conduct of the women do not determine the offence. In Ratinarayan Vs. State, 1992, Criminal Law journal, 269, 273, 273; See also, Khalandar Saheb Re, AIR 1955 SC 39, it was held that any act on the part of the person who lead a women astray from the path of rectitude is said to be seduction, and if it is followed by intercourse it will be seduction for illegal intercourse. If the girl is 18 or over she could be abducted not kidnapped but if she was under 18 years she could be abducted as well as kidnapped if the taking was by force or the taking or enticing was by deceitful means. For kidnapping by deceitful means, reference may be made to *Nawab Khan* Vs. State, where in the Supreme Court did not approve the conviction of the accused as the 'victim' who was for several days taken taken openly from place to place with out her protest when all the same she had opportunities to do so. The word forced is used in its ordinary sense and includes force by stress or circumstances. The expression seduced is used in Section 366(A) as inducing a women, to submit to illicit intercourse at any time. Where a girl under 18 years of age is taken the object of marriage or seduction, the accused shall be guilty of an offence of an offence notwithstanding the fact that the girl accompanied him of her own accord and not as a result of a force or misrepresentation. Sheltering Girls to illicit Intercourse is an offence as per section 366 of IPC. Where two girls under the age of 18 years ran away from their houses and remained for one or two days in a house of a woman of locality and no report was made to the police it was held that the woman in whose house the girls stayed was guilty of an offence under Section 366. Sections 366A, 366B are intended to punish the export and imports of girls for prostitution. Section 366A deals with procuration of minor girls from one part of India to another. As per section 366B it is an offence to import into India from any country outside India, girl below the age of 21 years for the purposes of prostitution.

Prostitution

The word Prostitution is not confined to acts of natural sexual intercourse but includes any act of lewdness. It means surrender of girls chastity for money. Section 372 of Indian Penal Code deals with regards to selling of minor for purposes of prostitution. This section applies to male or female under the age of 18 years. It applies to a married or an unmarried female even where such female prior to sale or purchase was leading an immoral life. It applies to a girl who is a member of the dancing girl caste. It is alarming that India has the highest number of Child Prostitute (more than 4 lakhs.) Suppression of Immoral Traffic in Women and Girls Act (SITA) was passed in 1956. It prohibits trafficking in human being and prohibit it near public places. According to SITA Prostitution is not illegal *per se*. The prostitute however can carry on her trade wherever she likes subject to certain restrictions. The purpose of the Act was to abolish or inhibit commercialized vice, namely the traffic in women and girls for purpose of prostitution as an organized means of living. However the idea was not to render prostitution a criminal offence or to punish a women merely because she prostitutes herself.

Immoral Traffic (Prevention) Act, 1986

In 1986 SITA was amended to do away with the loopholes that prevented it being effective. This Act was renamed Immoral Traffic (prevention) Act. Like its predecessor, this Act also does not declare prostitution illegal pre se. Under section 8 of the Act, the prostitute is treated as a criminal. Fortunately, this Act recognizes that children and even men can be sexually abused for commercial purposes and should be protected. Section 2 of this Act makes the definition of brothel wider to include any place used for the purpose of sexual exploitation or abuse. Section 9 provides for greater punishment to the persons who cause, aid or abet the seduction of women or girls over whom they have authority or who are in their care and custody for prostitution. The Act empowers the Central Government to appoint trafficking officers who can search without warrant any premises where this offence is suspected of being committed or being made to carry on.

Rape

Rape is one of the most reprehensible crimes and is often unreported. The legal meaning of term rape is the performance is the sexual act with a woman without her consent through force or use of force or fraud. Section 376 of the penal code provides that the rapists shall be punished with imprisonment of either description for a term which shall not be less than 7 years but which may extend to imprisonment for life or a term extending to 10 years with or without fine. Section 376 (2) of the Penal Code whoever carves out situation where more than the aforesaid punishment is intended to be awarded. These cases are those such as custodial rapes, i.e. by police officers within the limits of the police station where he is appointed or within the premises of the police station or rape by a public servant or officials of a jail, remand homes or places where woman and children are lodged in custody by whatever name called or in the hospital by the hospital staff. These are treated as more severe and awarded the minimum jail sentence of 10 years. Cases of gang rape are also seriously punished. It is strange In law that there is no separate section for Commission of the offence of attempt to rape like those of attempt to murder or attempt to commit suicide or robbery etc. The crime of rape is committed in secrecy. Under such circumstances, the statement of the victim assumes great importance and should not be discarded till there are overwhelming circumstances to rebut her charges.

The above analysis of legal provisions is just an attempt to sensitize the readers, especially women, in order to drive home the point that some tailor made legal courses are very essential for women who are otherwise literates. As it is said '*knowledge is power*' a bare minimum indoctrination of law and legal system for women would certainly pave the way for real empowerment of women with a renewed vigor and strength

Need for Legal Literacy

Legal literacy is in short knowledge of law of the land and constitutional arrangements that is imparted to the citizens by dispassionate and impartial agencies, be it the agencies enumerated in the legal authorities act 1987 or law schools or other bodies like NGO's. In normal parlance Legal education is basically understood in formal sense by reference to degrees such as B.L, LL.B, LL.M and so on so forth. Truly these legal qualifications are best available in the country. Law being a vast subject, it is not practical to reduce it to user friendly modules and impart legal education to women. Never the less the positive impact of informal legal literacy campaigns initiated by state and district legal services authorities for specific target groups of population are remarkable. Women's associations and feminist organizations are not lagging behind in this endeavor. However it is a fact that more than 90% of women who are otherwise educated with formal qualifications in various fields such as humanities, engineering, medicine etc. do not possess basic knowledge of law and legal system in the country. They have no choice but to consult a legal practitioner to help them out often more for curative purposes than for preventive ones. The later is always preferable to the former.

A question would arise in all thinking minds as to why not a provision for basic legal education be made in all the formal qualifying courses besides the regular curriculum of those courses. It is a pertinent question that needs to be addressed. Protection of law is not a simple process as is understood by many. Relief for a victim or a complainant can be secured, only subject to certain lawful requirements such as a formal complaint, locus standi, cause of action, nature of offence,relief sought etc.

In the absence of basic and rudimentary knowledge of these requirements the victim is all at sea in deciding the best course of action for personal protection of her and initiating action against the accused. It is also a fact that lack of the basic knowledge of these legal requirements renders an individual incapable to take preventive steps or to secure pre-emptive arrangements for self protection and to avoid any penal liability. For instance if a women is aware of the basic provision of prevention of domestic violence act, 2006 without a formal qualification of law, she can be in a better position to conduct herself in such a way so that she can take the benefit of the act and help the courts to impart justice in her favour in matters such as maintenance, protection home, claiming matrimonial home etc. etc. reliefs of this nature can be many. Hence the need for basic knowledge of law of the land to be imparted to women in all walks of life. As the formal legal education is lengthy and expensive a gender friendly course module can be structured for the benefit of women.

Some Important Suggestions

Legal literacy and women empowerment surely are complementary. The more a women is aware of the law in whatever way it is, the more she is empowered primarily for her own protection and for protection of her minor children,let alone seeking her other claims. Legal literacy would pave the way for self realization of women and would demystify the hoax of male chauvinism. Here are certain ways and means towards this end:

(a) Right from the middle school standard ie, eighth standard onwards, the basic concepts of three major acts i.e., Indian penal code, criminal procedure code, Indian evidence act can be taught especially to the girl students in all the schools as a part of curriculum.

(b) the content of basic legal education can be phased out up to graduation on a compulsory basis no matter what the regular faculty involved in, is.

(c) The legal literacy course of this nature can be of a qualifying nature with a bearing on the total aggregate of marks just as it is, in the case of languages.

(d) Practical exposure to court proceedings, police stations procedures, can be incorporated at the level of matriculation and higher secondary certificate examinations. This would help demystify the unwanted awe and fear of the uniform services (police).

(e) Special sessions on important case studies, leading cases on women issues can be conducted in order to instill confidence courage at practical level.

(f) Short term courses on basic legal knowledge can be conducted for working women irrespective of their nature of employment.

It is really surprising that no serious thought has gone in to this aspect of women empowerment, in any State in the country. Legal education has been tailor made as per the guidelines of Bar Council of India and the provisions of Advocates Act, 1961. The jurisprudence of the country is much wider and more superior to the laws and enactments made by the legislature. Legal literacy to women is surely a part of the great Indian tradition of jurisprudence right from the days of Mahabharata where we have Droupadi questioning on being summoned to court whether she was won by Kauravas before Yudhishter lost himself or after that. The epics and the history of India are full with many instances of argumentative power of women. Amartya Sen's '*Argumentative Indian*' throws ample light on this subject. It's high time the policy makers seriously ponder upon the suggestions that are made above in order to make the women of India truly empowered in its real sense.

7

Governance of Higher Education—Promoting Social Cohesion (Equity, Access and Inclusion)

Introduction

'The system, as a whole, is over-regulated but under-governed', the NKC commented in it's report in it's recommendations on Higher Education. I believe it is apt observation invariably true in majority of cases so far as the governance in higher education is concerned. The National Knowledge Commission has made recommendations on various aspects of higher education in India I, in all sincerity, believe that if all of them are taken seriously the scenario of education would dramatically change for better. Amongst many recommendations equity, access and inclusion are very important for these are the real areas of concerns for a meaningful system of higher education. The report of the NKC focused on the need for excellence in the system, expansion of the higher education and providing access for larger numbers of students. The gross enrollment ratio in the country today is less than 7% which is about half of that of entire Asia. The medium term macro objective with regard to higher education would be to increase the gross enrolment ratio to at least 15% by 2015. This surely appears to be a Herculean task given the sad state of ground realities. Majority of colleges and universities in the country are poorly equipped with necessary and basic infrastructural facilities such as buildings, libraries, class rooms, hostels, laboratories, auditoriums, play grounds etc.; let alone IT facilities with required bandwidth. It is any body's imagination as to how the lofty goals of equity, access and inclusion can be realized.

These three goals (equity, access and inclusion) are inter related and complimentary to each other. Inclusion takes place when access is ensured by simplifying the procedures and reaching out to hither to neglected sections people and geographical areas. This again is only possible when equity in favour of the neglected is incorporated in all policies of development, be it economic, social or political. Equity is the other side of the universal principles of Equality though it does not exactly restrict it self to such meaning. Justice and good conscience with an affirmative action for the uplift of all those neglected sections of people irrespective of caste, creed or language would largely explain the term. The denial of higher education or even the basic primary education, for that matter, to millions in this country for ages is no longer a secret. The picture today is not very heartening though, it is not worse either. A lot is yet to done.

The Need for Social Cohesion

Social cohesion is accommodation various interests with an underlying theme of peaceful coexistence. It is better ensured by a representative governance comprising of representatives from various stake holders. The concerns and secular interests of these stake holders are given adequate importance in such a system of governance. The concepts equity, access and inclusion will have true meaning even if the interests of all are looked after well though the physical representation is not completely practical. It is unfortunate that today that despite loud talk the university governance is far from representative. The system of appointment of Heads of institutions, members to various bodies, executive councils etc. is generally shrouded in the mystery of selection process where in all kinds of subjectivities sneak in turning the entire exercise in to a power game of politics. The politics creep in to such an extent that while nominating members from underprivileged sections also the compromising and less vigilant forces are preferred to belligerent and committed. It all appears as if it is all about more of political cohesion than social. The need of the hour is an effective and transparent system of appointments to various positions of decision making for is these decision makers who can make or mar things. It is a radical thought but certainly not impractical. The entire world of academicians, bureaucrats and public representatives should rise to the occasion.

The NKC laid emphasis on fundamental mechanisms for social inclusion through the creation of more opportunities for all deserving students proposing measures such as adopting a needs blind admissions policy, and well-funded and extensive National Scholarship Scheme targeting economically underprivileged students and historically socially disadvantaged groups. It also advocated for an Affirmative action to ensure that access to education for economically and historically socially underprivileged students The report says 'Disparities in educational attainments are related to caste and social groups, but are also strongly related to other indicators such as income, gender, region and place of residence. Therefore, we need to develop a meaningful and comprehensive framework that would account for the multi-dimensionality of differences that still persist.' A system of weighted score card was recommended by the commission.

The action, in the view of the Commission,for achieving the above ideals requires at three different levels: reforms within existing systems, changes in policies, and amendments in, or the introduction of, new statutes or legislation. Similarly implementation also is expected at three different levels: universities, state governments and the central government. It's here the concept of governance of higher education steps in. Let us take areas of concerns one by one and analyze the problems and possibilities with regard to social cohesion *vis a vis* governance of higher education.

Action for Access

Access is sine qua non for acquisition of knowledge and knowledge is life line for mankind. It is unfathomable, trans geographical and trans historical. One can not acquire knowledge independent of aids such as literature, libraries, pedagogy, and academic environment. The rural –urban divide is glaringly apparent because of the lack of these aids, be it economic, social, or cultural. The increasing migration of people from rural to urban is primarily due to this. Majority of colleges under a university in the country have neither all weather buildings, well equipped libraries, or adequate teaching staff. The result being poor enrollment and poor pass out ratio. The budgetary allocation are bismally incommensurate to the demands and needs. Quite often the MLAs and MPs of the area come to the rescue of institutions by donating sums from their funds such as MPLADS (Members of Parliamentary legislative Areas Development Sheme). The motives are guided by vote bank politics more often than not. Nevertheless the philanthropy behind the gesture must not be discredited. However what is needed is a more positive action from State. The increase of central budget for higher education in 11th plan is a relief. But it is n't enough as we *have miles to go before* we actually reap the intended fruits of the Access. The State Governments must develop workable time bound action plans in consultations with the Vice Chancellors in order to ensure priorities of infrastructure both physical and academic. It is a tragedy that in many States Departments of HE do not involve the University input agencies in finalizing the plans for under graduate education. The result, often, is mismatching of priorities. The, Bureaucrats, with all due respects, are generalists than specialists. Their tenure in the ministry is uncertain. It is important to note that actions taken or changes introduced in the system will have permanent impact on the stake holders for good or worse. The role of Vice Chancellors and Principals of colleges is very important in developing priorities and suggesting alternatives. The same should be encouraged in governance of higher education irrespective of time and space. Access is materialized by un bridled proliferation of aids of education and pedagogic communication. The tangible and permanent assets are necessary for equipping institutions of higher learning to enable them deliver results expected of Access. Academic road maps for Access are essential. The college drop outs of different age groups can also be made stake holders by reforming the enrollment procedures. The Bar Council of India's decision to bar the above *thirty* for admission in to law colleges is not an example for access. Such radical steps discourage the knowledge appetite.

According to Knowledge Commission the higher education system needs a massive expansion of opportunities, to the tune of 1500 universities nationwide, to enable India to attain a gross enrolment ratio of at least 15 per cent by 2015. The governance of Universities becomes more crucial in such an event for the existing number of Universities are considerably handicapped with governing problems. Though the access is provided through infrastructure poor governance may jeopardize the goals of access. The governance should facilitate the avenues for access by following best practices:

- Reduce procedural red tape and age old tricks of harassment to stake holders typical of *inspector raj*
- Pro active drive must be initiated for greater enrollment through mass communication
- Simplification of rules for recruitment of teaching staff and utilization of local pedagogic talents and resources
- Provision of greater financial out lays for libraries and subsidized reading materials

- better coordination between academicians and officers of the State/Ministry and larger involvement of representatives of affected sections of stake holders.

There is an increasing need for the above areas of intervention every where as the performance in these areas is pathetically discouraging.

Inclusion *vis-a-vis* Governance

The concept of inclusion as defined by UNESCO, involves the "transformation of schools and other centers of learning to cater for all children" and recognizes that many currently marginalized groups (such as religious, racial, ethnic, and linguistic minorities, immigrants, girls, the poor, students with disabilities, HIV/AIDS patients, remote populations, and more) are not actively included in education and learning processes. (UNESCO (2009) Policy Guidelines on Inclusion in Education. UNESCO: Paris) The thrust is on the idea that all students can learn and benefit from education irrespective of caste, creed, language or religion. The focus is on the learning with educational institutions adapting to the needs of students, rather than students adapting to the needs of the institution. Individual differences between students are to be utilized as a sources of richness and diversity, rather than magnifying them as problems. Inclusive education is a process of removing barriers and enabling all students, including previously excluded groups, to learn and participate effectively within general institutional systems and mechanisms.

The administration of academic institutions needs to be so tuned and modified that the hither to sections left out owing to various systemic constraints are encouraged to participate with out restraints. There requires a golden mean to be struck between rigid rules generated academic compulsions and the demands of social cohesion guided by equity and good conscience. After all we live in a welfare State and not in a state of *live and let die* of laissez-faire.

C.V. Ramans, Lincolns, or Ambedkars can not be taken as often quoted examples to prove excellence by individual efforts amidst economic and social hardships. Celebrity geniuses can not always come from ghettos of poverty. Today the State has a responsibility to look after the needs of its citizens and provide for the same. Chapter 4 of the Constitution is complementary to Chapter 3. Directive Principle are enshrined in the document to remind the State that the fundamental Rights can be meaningful only by imlipenting the Directive Principles.

In India it is a fact that Institutions of higher learning never look in the fact that how their feeder cadre i.e the students of High Schools and plus two institutions, are placed in nook and corners of the country. There is a large gap between system of collegiate teaching and that of Schools. The results are academic shocks as the standards of different schools from where the intake is drawn are never the same with enormous diversity of regions, languages and incomes, to name a few. The general fall out is dilution in quality. Inclusion becomes meaningful only when these gaps are bridged and a smooth change over to new environment. Here becomes the role of governance very challenging.

Inclusion will be incomplete if we do not discuss the gender budgeting - the trend of the day. Women constitute half of the world's and India is fortunately no exception. But the issue to be addressed is whether we are adequately sensitized it this regard. How many Universities out of 350 in the country are exclusively for women? Or is academic sex ratio is commensurate to that of Census ? We need to go a long way, I am afraid, to answer these questions satisfactorily. Gender budgeting is not transparent in academic world. The general status of Women in our country is no different form that of other under privileged or oppressed sections of Society irrespective of their caste or faith. As a result often Access becomes *sour grapes* for them, for they are denied the same either in the name of latent protectionism or manifest discrimination by male dominated families. The syndrome is so rampant at Primary level that only a semblance of representation is all that is left at the level of higher learning. An occasional visit to Colleges and Universities will vouch for the fact saving the trouble of organizing academic Census. The number women students is not in proportion to the figures of women population in the Country. The Administration of higher education must address this issue. Let us not forget *'the hand that rocks the cradle rules the world'*. Here are certain does for Inclusion illustratively :

(*a*) The Governance must create inclusion friendly systems such as bridge courses or make up curriculums for benefit of the stake holders for level playing.

(*b*) Identification of stake holders for inclusion has to be designed with a provision of weight age for different handicaps.

(*c*) Exclusive women friendly admission procedures and facilities are to be created to draw more intake, breaking social and family barriers.

(*d*) Effective representation of women in decision making bodies of higher learning must be ensured. Gender budgeting is a must.

(*e*) A gender based concession could be introduced in evaluation system of examination for an positive encouragement for more inclusion of women.

(*f*) Creation of residential infrastructure for the stake holders besides academic affluence.

The above illustrative steps may help as Guide lines to the pundits of governance of HE.

Separation of Academic and Administrative functions would do a lot of good in this regard. The Central Board of Undergraduate Education along with State Boards of Undergraduate Education as proposed by the National

Knowledge Commission would set curricula and conduct examinations for undergraduate colleges that choose to be affiliated with them. These Boards would thus separate the academic functions from the administrative functions and at the same time provide quality benchmarks. Governance would thus become separate and much simpler. The problems of inclusion can be effectively addressed by the proposed Boards as they are intended to be independent Body Corporate far from the influence of vested interests. The above suggestions can be better looked in to by these bodies as the administrative functions are separate from academic ones. The regular governance of institutions will confine it self exclusively to issues of structural arrangements such as infrastructure, budgeting and preparation and supervision of Acton plans.

Equity as the Heart and Soul of Society

Inclusion is a challenging concept for it involves he principles of Equity. Equity is a notion that emanates from the conscience of human beings in a civilized society where the human rights are recognized and protected, no matter whether they are constitutionally guaranteed or legally provided or institutionally safeguarded. Equity is more wider than the concept of equality for in the latter the pre existence of legal rights are essential where as in the former it is not material. Many a time the Human Rights are violated in practice as the State can not all the time pro actively step in to ensure them in the absence of the voice of the affected. Equity comes in here. In general we can say that Equity is a principal of natural justice that ensures relief to the deprived individuals or sections of people whom the established Law can not protect otherwise as the complexities of legal frame work does not allow. In the field of higher education the concept of Equity is deeply enrooted in the form of Protective discrimination and affirmative action, be it the reduction of cut off mark for admissions, be it Scholarships or be it accommodation in the Hostels.

However there are still certain areas of concern left out unaddressed. For instance the geographical and economic disparities, the rural urban inequalities or the Physical or mental handicaps in the stake holders are some areas of focus for Equity.

The governance must keep in mind that Equity can not be sacrificed for the sake of rules and regulations. We can not *'throw the baby with the bath water'*. After all education is not for the sake of education ; it is for the mankind. The concept of *Vasudeva Kutumbakam* is a path finder. Adequate considerations are to be given for the stake holders with the formally un acknowledged but practically evident inequalities and injustices. The academic rigidities do not accommodate genuine but unexpressed claims of such sections of people. We need following safeguards are sine qua non to this end:

- The budgeting has to be equity driven and accommodative of un protected secular interests.
- Representation of the sections in need of Equity must be ensured both in academics and in administration.
- Special initiatives such as concessions or affirmative actions need to be launched for the protection of the stake holders. For example, physically handicapped, widows, aboriginal tribes, Children of War victims, minorities etc. etc.
- Constant monitoring of the effects of the affirmative actions to be ensured by independent assessment agencies.

Equity is the mother of equality. The institutions of higher learning should embody these universal principles in their thoughts and actions in the matters of governance.

Conclusion

Social cohesion is a democratic concept backed by the philosophy of pluralistic society where interests of all sections of people are given due importance in decision making. Governance in higher education need to positively consider the social factors such as caste, religion, language, economic status of stakeholders i.e. the target groups for learning. Social harmony is undoubtedly better ensured by changing the age old divisive mind set of people which can only be achieved by spread of higher education. It is important to bear in mind that we mean higher education and not primary/ school education because the former is a higher form of learning with higher content that can demystify the traditional oppressive ideologies which divided the society and endangered the unity and cohesion for centuries.

Higher education needs to be imparted to all sections of society with out barriers of procedures and policies often perpetrated by traditional systems of governance. The administration of institutions of higher learning has to be democratic and rational in making decisions that effect millions of stake holders. What is imperative here is the adherence to social needs and demands for education is not just for education's sake; it is to bring about a social change in order to create a united, secular and democratic India as opposed to a colonial dominion. Let us not forget that it is the education that our fore fathers had during the *Raj* that created a consciousness for freedom and the result is that here we are today –a free and republican India. Hence the need for a proper governance in managing the institutions if we need to have a socially cohesive India.

Transparency, fair play and objectivity are hallmarks of an effective system of governance in academic institutions. Our efforts will be incomplete if we do not include the role of E-governance the trend of the day. Max Weber, the protagonist of modern bureaucracy would have been the happiest man, had he been alive, to see the checks and balances introduced by E-governance. Nothing could be more transparent and accountable than E-governance. Universities, colleges and institutions have an impending necessity to switch over to E-governance systems, and procedure in place of obsolete paper work rigmarole. It is no more a secret that systems like biometrics, smart cards and on line interface ensure total transparency and accountability in academic functions. All procedures can be made paperless. It is time that governance in higher education went high tech in all aspects. The IT sector is a catalyst for social change for it facilitates speed in communication and reach of knowledge to masses in the least expensive way.

Modernity signifies two elements of universal wisdom, namely rationality and secularism. Both these being bed rocks of social change are realised only by an effective system of higher learning. The governance of higher learning should be such as to play the pivotal role in modernising the Indian Tradition. Social cohesion will be a natural corollary of such an adventurous governance. On the other hand it will be terrible if the other way round happens with undemocratic and autocratic governing elite, that is Modernity getting traditionalised. (refer for conceptual clarity *'Modernization of Indian Tradition'* by *M.N. Srinivas*) We must caution our selves against such a pathetic eventuality. After all, the entire exercise is to build a modern India. Hence the need to modernize the governance it self to begin with. The ideals of Equity, the demands of Access and the need for Inclusion get fully realised only through a system of modern governance not only in letter but in spirit too.

It is often seen that Universities, practically, function as intellectual islands or as academic forts living in *'splendid isolation'* (The Monroe Doctrine during second world war). They remember the affiliated colleges only in times of examinations. The academic activities in colleges are usually carried on with out supervision by the Universities. The problems such as quality in pedagogic exercise or in governance of under graduate institutions persist eternally. As the apex body of academics the Universities have greater responsibility in caring and nurturing the colleges. The systems of governance must address this area of concern. Degrees and certificates are just not meant to be testimonials of individual academic prowess to secure a living. Rather they are to remind the individuals that they are entrusted with a unique responsibility to initiate social change. This is possible by not only a good governance but also by an accountable modern governance.

8
Protective Discrimination and Equality before Law

Introduction

The issue of protective discrimination otherwise popularly known as reservations in jobs and academic institutions has always been a controversial subject for the policy makers in the country. Fundamental rights are a part of the *basic structure* of the Constitution of India. In various cases the Supreme Court of India has categorically laid down that any amendment to the Constitution should not disturb the basic structure whereby it is very clear that fundamental rights are not to be adversely affected, at any cost, by any law, however strongly backed by the needs of the society or even by the Constitutional provisions, for that matter. Nevertheless it is generally observed that the first amendment made in article 15 (4) way back in 1951 aimed at making special provisions for the advancement of socially, educationally backward communities or SC's and ST's is taken as a shelter for perpetuating caste based or community based reservation in the country. This has a strong detrimental impact on the objectives of article 14 where in right to equality and equal protection of law have been enshrined. It is a paradox that on one hand article 14 envisages equality before law while on the other article 15(4) takes away the fruits of the same.

It is observed quite a few non SC/ST castes have been transforming themselves in to pressure groups and, either by lawful or by unlawful ways and means, have been trying to over awe the state to secure the so called reservations in jobs and educational institutions. Such a tendency has unfortunately been on the rise for the last couple of decades. The determination of these communities is so firm that many a time their agitations paralyze even the democratic civilian life in various parts of the country. The Gurjar agitation in Rajasthan is a glaring example of the severity of this sort of outbursts.

The basic and the pertinent question that should arise in the minds of law makers is whether violence and agitation could become a source of law. Equally important question that surface is in the nationalistic minds is whether the fundamental rights guarantied truly and effectively stand up, in letter and spirit, to the expectations of an average citizen. Or is it just a convenient process of law making by interpreting article 14 and 15(4) to suit the respective needs of respective communities throttling the essence of preamble and the soul of the Constitution?. This is the crux of the subject under question.

The socio-legal aspects of law making process should lead to democratically acceptable alternatives to the issue of caste based reservation. In short the complicated political process of reservation laws must be replaced by a better and practical approach for the upliftment of under privileged communities. Effective guaranties and equitable provisions can be made as alternatives to caste based reservations so that the spirit of article 14 can be kept alive and the downtrodden communities can be made economically independent, socially equal and politically decisive. The entire law making process in this respect can be given a new dimension and a new direction to achieve this end.

The Heart and Soul of the Constitution

Undoubtedly the Constitution of India is a unique piece of master draftsmanship for it is the most well written document meant for the governance and preservation of the democratic society of India with an underlying sentiment of national unity and integrity. The preamble speaks the essence and spirit of the Indian Constitution.

> *"We the people of India, having solemnly resolved to constitute India in to a Soveriegn, Socialist, Secular, Democratic, Republic and secure to all it's citizens:*
>
> *Justice, social, economic and political Liberty of thought, expression, belief, faith and worship Equality of status and opportunity and to promote among them all fraternity ensuring dignity of individual and the unity and integrity of the nation :"*

The preamble is the heart and soul of the Constitution. However in 'Berubari Case'[1] the Bench has unanimously observed that the only purpose of preamble was to show the general purpose for which the makers of the Constitution made the enacting provisions in the Constitution.......' it couldn't be regarded as an independent source of any substantive power or prohibition'. It was observed that preamble was not a part of the Constitution'. But in 'Kesawananda Bharati'[2] case the preamble was considered a part of basic features of Constitution for the objectives specified in preamble indicate basic structure. 7 out of 13 judges in 'Kesawanda' held that the objective specified in the preamble contain the basic structure of our Constitution, which can not be amended in exercise of the power under article 368. It is very important to note that in G.C. Kanungo Vs. State of Orissa[3] it was held that judicial power of the state exercisable by the courts under the Constitution as sentinels of rule of law is a basic feature of the Constitution. 'But' it was held in Registrar(admn.) Vs. Sisir Kant Satpathy[4] the said power has to be excercised with in four corners of the Constitution and not beyond that.".

In Ashok Kumar Gupta Vs. State of U.P.[5] it was observed that the S.C. is not bound to accept an interpretation which retards the progress and impedes social integration, it adopts such interpretation which would bring about the ideas set down in the preamble aided by part III (fundamental rights) and IV (directive principles of state policy) of Constitution.

In Balbir Kaur Vs. SAIL[6] it was also held that the Constitutional philosophy should be allowed to become a part of every man's life and the socialistic pattern of society envisaged in the Constitution has to be attributed its full meaning.

It is very intriguing that on one hand the basic structure which includes fundamental rights inter alia is often effected as and when the State make legislations of protective discrimination in favor of certain under privileged castes or Communities. Article 14 and 15 lay down the principles of secular and democratic society by ensuring equality before law, equal protection of law and by prohibiting discrimination on the grounds of religion, race, caste, sex or place of birth. Nevertheless Article 15(4) enables state to seek exemption from article 15(2) and 29(2) in enacting laws of protective discrimination in favor of any socially and educationally backward classes of citizen or for the SC/ST, for their advancement. The result is, today 49.5% of jobs and educational opportunities are reserved for different castes, and interestingly more and more socially specific groups are battling lawfully and unlawfully for the same treatment. The question then arises as to what and where is this basic structure (Kesawanda)' and how the words 'Secular, Democratic, Republic' are to be reinterpreted.

The sources of law had never been agitations with violence, destruction of life and property. But today it appears that law making has become more political than democratic and least so secular to speak. Article 15(4) was introduced with the first amendment to Constitution in the year 1951. It was meant as an exception to article 15(2) for making certain legislations for the advancement of weaker sections of Indian society. Article 14 and article 15(4) are apparently contradictory and against the expression 'Secular' in the preamble. However the word 'socialist' might clear the ambiguity. But yet it remains to be answered as to how long the effect of 15(4) is to remain in relation to art. 14 where in the fundamental right of 'equality before law' is secured. The basic apprehension in the minds of citizens of India would be about the imminent and invisible threat to the 'basic structure' of the Constitution in a given situation where in the art. 15(4) is used as convenient recourse for any legislation to appease or placate the warring groups for reservations of different types at different levels in the name of caste.

It is no denying that the socially educationally backward castes and scheduled castes and tribes need encouragement to join the main stream of Indian Society in it's all fields of development. Or else the 'socialist' phrase of the preamble would be rendered meaningless. Nevertheless such a protective discrimination has to be qualified with time and space. Even the Chairman of the drafting committee of the constitution, Dr. Ambedkar was never in favor of a perpetual positive discrimination and least so with regard to job reservations. As a great visionary he emphasized on ownership of means of production in the hands of the down trodden as a means towards economic independence and consequently social respect and dignity. In an exact opposite situation an eternal special privilege in favor of some, in due course of time would invariably relegate the so called upper castes of today to a status of down trodden some day, and that would result in a vicious circles; one community given privileges and the other discouraged and the latter given the same protection later on.., and so on so forth. This will have law making an instrument of political battle which can mutilate the concept of democratic legislation. Hence the need for a deep study on the relevance of reservation laws vis a vis the spirit of the constitution.

Criteria for Backwardness

Reservations in favor of backward castes has become a fait accompli. It is interesting to note that the Constitution of India has not mentioned what a backward caste is nor did defines what a backward class is. Though Art. 15(4) makes a provision that "Nothing in this Arti. (15) or in Clause (2) of Art. 29 shall prevent the State for making any special provision for the advancement of any socially and educationally backward classes of citizens or for the Scheduled Caste and the Scheduled Tribes", no criteria has been avowedly laid down either in Art. 16(4) or in Art. 340. Article 340 confers the powers of appointing a commission to investigate the conditions of backward classes. In exercise of the power conferred by Art. 340, read with the observations made by the 9-Judges Bench in *Indra's case (See Indra Sawhney v. Union of India, (1992) Supp. (3) SCC 217 (paras 652-54): AIR 1993 SC 477.)* Parliament has enacted the National Commission for Backward Classes Act, 1993 *(Vide App. II, post)* for the identification of the backward classes referred to in Cl. (4) of Art. 16, and to make special provisions relating to such backward classes and their reservations for appointment or posts under the Government of India.

The main provisions of this Act are:

(a) The constitution of this National Commission is left to the Central Governments.3(1)].

(b) The initial identification is also left to the Central Government by the words "such backward classes of citizens other than the Scheduled Castes and Scheduled Tribes as may be specified by the Central Government" [s.2(a)]. But applications for inclusion of other classes in the lists so made by the Central Government and the hearing of complaints relating to such lists shall be function of the Commission and though its function is advisory, its advice shall ordinarily be binding upon the Central Government [s. 9], and when the Government does not accept any such advice, the Government has to report such reasons to Parliament [s. 15]

(c) Lists of backward classes as aforesaid, shall be revised by the Central Government at the expiration of every ten years from the date of commencement of this Act, i.e., 1-2-1993, and such revision shall be made by the Government in consultation with the Commission [s. 11]

The above scheme of identification of beneficiaries creates tremendous political mileage. The judiciary is not left with any acceptable indices either. The practice of the courts has been to condone various criteria based on occupation and high school standards. Note for example, the following cases:

- *Balaji* (1963)[7] – (average of student population in lat three high school classes)
- *Chitralekha (*1964)[8] – (occupation cum income criteria)
- *P. Rajendran* (1968) [9] – (caste)
- *Minor A. Peeriakaruppan* (1971)[10] – (caste)
- *Balaram* (1972)[11] – (average student population in standards 10 and 11)
- *Janaki Prasad Parimoo* (1973)[12] – (occupation, commumity (artisans) and residence)
- *Pradip Tandon* (1975)[13]– (region)
- *KS Jayashree* (1976)[14] – (education levels upto matriculation or standadrd 10)
- However, the court rejected criteria based solely on caste in:
- *P. Sagar* (1968)[15]

The above are some of the important observations made by the apex court of the country that would help us to acquire a dispassionate understanding as what the issues involved in protective discrimination towards Backward classes are.

Determination of backward class has been left to be discretion of the State primarily because the indices that define backwardness are actually variables. It is practically impossible to lay down a hard and fast rule eliminating any scope to include the dynamic nature of society. Or else backwardness would become an instrument of political blackmail in the event of a demographically restricted criteria roping in specific castes. It would be a chronic malady that people would cling on to backwardness and would never try to achieve social and economic mobility upwards. Social backwardness is to be understood in consonance with economic backwardness. For instance a caste which is socially regarded has twice borne may actually be economically backward whereas the converse juxtaposition is practically impossible to imagine. Looking into inequal structure of Indian caste society the once borne have never been in the possession of the means of production as they were scribed only menial and service related occupations in the entire history. Hence it is all the more important that the social status of caste is to be taken into account in addition to economic backwardness. It should be borne in mind that intention of article 15(4) or 16(4) is not to make a class legislation. The aim is to make classified legislation by an objective criteria with regard to social and economic backwardness. The articles do not mention the word caste where by it is beyond any confusion that the goal of the legislation is not to make legislation in favour of a particular caste. On the contrary it is the class which has to be the yard stick in determining economic and social backwardness. *Because all classes are castes but all castes are not classes.*

A positive Law has to be objective in nature, devoid of any arbitrariness. Law should be legitimate endowed with the spirit of natural justice in consonance with rule of Law.

The framers of the constitution and successive parliaments have taken enough care and precaution to ensure that articles 15-(4) and 16(4) would only remain as exception and not become rules. Rules may be exempted but exemptions cannot become rules. Unfortunately the trend in modern India is towards the achieving the letter at the expense of the former. This is the root of the socially enomy and pertinent reason for civic strife. Unfortunately the exceptions in clauses (4) to article 15 and 16 have become almost fundamental rights in as much as the protection guaranteed against the compliance of the same is concerned. Secondly there is no state machinery evolved as yet which can monitor the effects of the protective discrimination given to backward classes (castes) and assess whether all classified target groups have taken advantage of the provision or is it only a minority that has benefited and still continue to do so not withstanding the fact that social backwardness no longer remains in its favour. In short the social and economic backwardness is often sustained or perpetrated rather than eliminated, ironically. It is also a fact that among this classified groups there is a vast majority with typical identities that have not tasted the fruits of concessions.

Some Challenging Proposition for the Policy Makers

In the light of the above assessment a few important questions about law, law making, equality, and liberty will surface in the minds of common men for whose welfare and growth the very process of law making is meant for.

1. Is there an alternative to reservation laws that are based on birth and community ?
2. Can equality under article 14 of the Constitution be guaranteed in true spirit and letter without compromising the philosophy behind the amendment (15(4)) of the Constitution in favour of caste reservations?

3. Can effective legislation be made in order to ensure socialistic pattern by ensuring the rights of the under privileged castes in the means of production and in democratic and secular society without thwarting the basic concept of 'equality before law'?
4. Can the republican form of government and state be so modified and restructured as to make the article 15(4) redundant or superfluous? What legal remedies can be restored in that direction?
5. Can Law establish an equality based social structure without making special provisions for a few to the detriment of the rest ?

The above questions are very crucial in as much as the basic process of law making on reservation is concerned, for they would suggest the ways and means to tackle the issue of equality versus inequality. The outcome of the exercise would be, in all probability, an emergence of a new thought and methodology which can help to understand better the issues involved. The answer to these questions lies in the strong political will to legislate effectively to strike a balance between part 3 and part 4 of the constitution. In other words the fundamental rights and the directive principles should truly be made complimentary to each other. Law making should not be made an instrument of politics or the vice versa. It will be impossible to suggest detailed alternatives in piece of writing as this. Nevertheless we can suggest that a clear blend of Equity, justice and good conscience in the intention of legislature will do good enough to repair the damages. Equality is nothing but equal opportunity; and that is ensured only by removing inequalities, be it economic, be it social, or be it regional or gender based. Innumerable pieces of enactments including the constitutional guarantees are in existence across the length and breadth of the country only meant to remove the inequalities as referred above. All that is required is their effective delivery system. An additional provision of protracted protective discrimination in the shape of a law would only create vicious circle of unending inequalities. After all where is the End and how static is the *main stream.*

References

1. Berubari VOI AIR 1960 SC 845 (856):1960 (3)SCR 250.
2. Kesavananda Bharati V State of Kerala, AIR 1973 SC 146 (paras 302, 509, 1437): (1973)4 SCC 225.
3. G.C. Kanungo V State of Orissa, (1995) 5 SCC 96 (paras 17& 18): AIR 1995 SC 1655.
4. Registrar Admn. V Sisir Kant Satapathy, (1999)7 SCC 725 (paras 1 & 2): AIR 1999 SC 3265.
5. Ashok Kumar Gupta V State of U.P., (1997) 5 SCC 201 (para 51).
6. Balbir Kaur V S.A.I.L., (2000)6 SCC 493 (para 8&9).
7. 1963 Supp (1) SCR 439 at 463.
8. (1964) 6 SCR 368 at 386-8.
9. (1968 2 SCR 786.
10. (1971) 1 SCC 38.
11. (1972) 1 SCC 660 at para 71.
12. (1973) 1 SCC 420.
13. (1975) 1 SCC 267.
14. (1976) 3 SCC 730 at 734-5.
15. (1968) 3 SCR 595.

9

Criteria for Social and Educational Backwardness : A Review

It is very important to have an understanding of protective discrimination granted for the advancement of socially and educationally backward classes of citizens or Scheduled Caste and Scheduled Tribes as provided in Art. 15 and Art. 16.

Art. 15(1) is a fundamental right against discrimination on the grounds only of religion, race, caste, sex, place of birth or any of them, while clause 4 is a provision as an exception for the advancement of socially and educationally backward classes or Scheduled Caste and Scheduled Tribes. Similarly Art. 16 positively gives a fundamental right for equality of opportunity in matters relating to employment or appointment to any office under the state. The protection against discrimination on the grounds of religion, race, caste, sex, descent, place of birth, residence or any of them, specially with regard to employment under the state, while the same protection is guaranteed by the constitution in Art. 15 with regard to general life and liberty to live.

It is significant to note, though Art. 15 and 16 have not defined what a backward class is or what a Scheduled Caste and Scheduled Tribe is. The underline theme in the above two fundamental rights with their exceptions as discussed above is not only to ensure equality before law and equal protection of law but also to provide special opportunities for those classes of citizens to be equal to obtain the benefits of these two fundamental rights in comparison with the relatively better off citizens of the country who do not suffer from the backwardness as visualized by Art. 15(4). In a case (1) It was held that preferential treatment of backward class and Scheduled Caste and Scheduled Tribes is a rational classification and is indeed necessary to make effective the equality of opportunity for all citizens which is provided by Art. 16(1).

Scope of Cl.(4) : Special Provision for Backward Classes

The object of this clause, added in 1951, is to bring Arts. 15 and 29 in line with Arts. 16(4), 46 and 340, and to make it constitutional for the State to reserve seats for backward classes of citizens, Scheduled Castes and Tribes, in the public educational institutions, as well as to make other special provisions as may be necessary for their advancement. But would not support the distribution of seats according to communities so as to discriminate between classes who are not backward, *inter se*. It is an exception to Cl. (1)[1] in so far as it forbids discrimination on the ground of 'race' or 'caste. However it cannot be so extended as to destroy the guarantee in Cl(1.).[2] Art. 15(4 envisages the policy of compensatory or protective discrimination but it should be reasonable and consistent with ultimate public interest i.e. national interest and the interest of community or society as a whole.[3] Article 15(4) and Art. 16(4) are enabling provisions and naturally does not create any fundamental rig ht and cannot ignore the fundamental rights of the rest of the citizens in favor of a member of the classes specified in Art. 14.[4] Art. 15(4) must, therefore, strike a reasonable balance between several relevant considerations and proceed objectively.[5]

Art. 340 —The Backward Castes Commission

It is interesting to note that the Constitution of India has not mentioned what a backward caste is nor did defines what a backward class is. Though Art. 15(4) makes a provision that "Nothing in this Art. (15) or in Clause (2) of Art. 29 shall prevent the State for making any special provision for the advancement of any socially and educationally backward classes of citizens or for the Scheduled Caste and the Scheduled Tribes", no criteria has been avowedly laid down either in Arti 16(4) or in Arti 340. Article 340 confers the powers of appointing a commission to investigate the conditions of backward classes. In exercise of the power conferred by Art. 340, read with the observations made by the 9-Judges Bench in *Indra's case (See Indra Sawhney v. Union of India,(1992) Supp. (3) SCC 217 (paras 652-54): AIR 1993 SC 477.)* Parliament has enacted the National Commission for Backward Classes Act, 1993 *(Vide App. II, post)* for the identification of the backward classes referred to in Cl. (4) of Art. 16, and to make special provisions relating to such backward classes and their reservations for appointment or posts under the Government of India.

Test of Backward Classes

1. It is to be noted that while Art. 16(4) simply mentions any backward class of citizens', Art. 15(4) the class must be both socially and educationally backward.[6] Thus, mere educational backwardness is not enough if the class is not socially backward, and vice versa.

The Scheduled Castes and Tribes can be enumerated by a Presidential Order while there is no such provision for members of the backward classes which means that they cannot be specified by enumeration, but must be determined by applying objective tests.[7]

The social backwardness which results from poverty is likely to be aggravated by considerations of caste but the classification of backwardness cannot be made solely on the basis of caste,[8].Caste is, of course, *one* of the relevant circumstances in determining backwardness, but if a group has been classified as backward on other relevant considerations,[9] that classification cannot be challenged. If, the criterion adopted for determining their backwardness is fictitious; it would not be protected by C.(4) and would be hit by Cl.(1).[10]

If a caste, as a whole, if found to be socially and educationally backward, the inclusion of such caste in the list of backward classes would not be violative Art. 15(4),[11] even though a few individuals in that case may be socially and educationally above the average.[12] The test of backwardness had always been a controversial exercise. Both in pre constitutional era from 1880 to 1950 and in post constitutional period till date different criteria, by different successive governments at different stages, were adopted in advocating reservations for backward classes. Caste and class were given synonymous interpretations to fit the beneficiaries in to the criteria. Even the so called "twice born" castes were treated as backward. When social and economic backwardness is not transparent enough to agree upon with consensus with relation to Hindu Caste society it can not be ruled out that subjectivity sneaks in the process of law making to the detriment of the spirit of art 14 and 15. It is not certainly the case with Scheduled Castes and Tribes as the sole criteria in this is Untouchability.

In the absence of a definition of the expression in the Constitution, the determination of which classes are 'backward' is left to the 'state' as defined in Art. 12[13] It is open to the State to act according to the advice of the Backward Classes Commission [Art. 340]. The Determination by such Commission does not become invalid on the ground that the Commission has used its personal knowledge for the purpose of charactering a group as backward.[14]

According to justice Pasayat who passed the interim order[15] injuncting the implementation of the Central Educational Insstitutions (Reservation of Admission) Act, 2007 the evidence that had to be examined was overwhelming. He asked: "*Was the Act enacted on a basis of unfounded and unsupportable data about the number of* OBCs.[16] In reply, it was urged that "*(t)here never has been any determination of (OBCs) on any accepted basis.*"[17] What was put in evidence was the National Sample Survey Organisation (NSSO), the Sumitra Mahajan Standing Committee of Parliament on Social Justice and Empowerment, the Annual Report of the National Commission of Backward Classes and the Report of the (Moily) Oversight Committee constituted under the orders of the Prime Minister on 27th July 2006.[19]

The Court tentatively but firmly concluded that[19]

"(t)here is no dispute and in fact it was fairly accepted by the learned Additional Solicitor General that there is need for periodical identification of the backward citizens and for this purpose the need for survey of entire population on the basis of an acceptable mechanism.[20]

It followed: "Differentiation or classification for special preference must not be unduly unfair for the persons left out of the favour groups.[21] *Nor could any policy "perpetuate backwardness.*[22] *Nagaraj's case was relied on in the interest of the creamy layer*[23] *with the creamy layer being seen "as a necessary bargain between caste based reservation and the principle of secularism.*[24]

The practice of the courts has been to condone various criteria based on occupation and high school standards. Note for example, the following cases:

- *Balaji* (1963)[25] – (average of student population in lat three high school classes)
- *Chitralekha* (1964)[26] – (occupation cum income criteria)
- *P. Rajenddran* (1968)[27] – (caste)
- *Minor A. Peeriakaruppan* (1971)[28] – (caste)
- *Balaram* (1972)[29] – (average student population in standards 10 and 11)

- *Janaki Prasad Parimoo* (1973)[30] – (occupation, commumity (artisans) and residence)
- *Pradip Tandon* (1975)[31] – (region)
- *KS Jayashree* (1976)[32] – (education levels upto matriculation or standadrd 10)

However, the court rejected criteria based solely on caste in:

- *P. Sagar* (1968)[33]

The above are some of the important observations made by the apex court of the country that would help us to acquire a dispassionate understanding as what the issues involved in protective discrimination towards Backward classes are.

Determination of backward class has been left to be discretion of the State primarily because the indices that define backwardness are actually variables. It is practically impossible to lay down a hard and fast rule eliminating any scope to include the dynamic nature of society. Or else backwardness would become an instrument of political blackmail in the event of a demographically restricted criteria roping in specific castes. It would be a chronic malady that people would cling on to backwardness and would never try to achieve social and economic mobility upwards. Social backwardness is to be understood in consonance with economic backwardness. For instance a caste which is socially regarded has twice borne may actually be economically backward whereas the converse juxtaposition is practically impossible to imagine. Looking into unequal structure of Indian caste society the once borne have never been in the possession of the means of production as they were ascribed only menial and service related occupations in the entire history. Hence it is all the more important that the social status of caste is to be taken into account in addition to economic backwardness. It should be borne in mind that intention of article 15(4) or 16(4) is not to make a class legislation. The aim is to make classified legislation by an objective criteria with regard to social and economic backwardness. The articles do not mention the word caste which clarifies beyond any confusion that the goal of the legislation is not to make legislation in favor of a particular caste. On the contrary it is the class which has to be the yard stick in determining economic and social backwardness. *Because all classes are castes but all castes are not classes.*

Exclusion of 'Creamy Layer' from Reservation

The majority Judges in Indra Sawhney case observed: "The very concept of a class denotes a number of persons having certain common traits which distinguish them from the others. In a backward class under Clause (4) of Article 16, if the connecting link is the social backwardness, it should broadly be the same in a given class. If some of the members are far too advanced socially (which in the context, necessarily means economically and may also mean educationally) the connecting thread between them and the remaining class snaps. They would be misfits in the class. After excluding them alone, would the class be a compact class? In fact, such exclusion benefits the truly backward."

The concept of creamy layer as laid down by the Supreme Court is a very important yardstick designed to ensure justice for those stake holders with in the OBC who are not the cream. In a way it is measuring rod to protect the backwards from with in.

Following the Supreme Court judgement in the case of *Indira Sawhney and others vs. Union of India and others*[34] Govt. appointed an Expert Committee to recommend criteria for exclusion of socially advanced persons/sections from the benefits of reservations for the backward classes. The Creamy layer guidelines were developed by the Expert Committee for specifying the criteria for identification of socially advanced persons among the socially and educationally backward classe. This Committee was headed by Justice (retired) R N Prasad, and submitted its report on 10.3. 93. On the basis of this report, the Government of India issued the guidelines to define the 'Creamy layer' Consequent thereto, the scheme of reservation of OBCs, was modified as under[35]

(i) The 27% reservation for OBCs shall not apply to persons/sections mentioned in the Schedule to O.M. No. 36012/22/93-Estt. (SCT), dt. 8.9.1993.

(ii) However, persons working as artisans or engaged in hereditary occupations, callings notified by the Min. of Welfare, shall not be excluded under the criteria at (i) above.

(iii) The criteria for determining Creamy Layer status of sons and daughters of persons in Government services, or of persons holding equivalent or comparable posts in PSUs, Banks, Insurance been laid down in the Schedule to DOPT, O.M. No. 36012/22/93-Estt. (SCT), dt. 8.9.1993 (Annexure 21.8)------------------------

(iv) The creamy layer status of the sons and daughters of employees of organizations where evaluation of the posts on equivalent or comparable basis basis has not been made is determined on the basis of 'Income/Wealth Tax'. Accordingly, children of persons having gross annual income (excluding income from salaries or agricultural land) of Rs. 2.5 lakhs or above or possessing wealth above the exemption limit as per Wealth Tax Act (presently Rs. 15 lacs) for a period of three consecutive years would be treated as falling in creamy layer.[36]

(v) However, children of parents who have suffered permanent incapacitation shall not be treated as to fall in creamy layer in certain circumstances [37]

The Defects in the Criteria

The Concept of 'Creamy Layer' is theoretically very important and is meant to be a trend setter. The exclusion of the 'creamy layer' together with some reservations for economically weaker sections constitute actually an important complement to the principle which integrates holistically all sections of the OBC and the non-OBC poor. It is this unity which will sustain the struggle to eliminate the existing social and economic inequality. However the aim and purpose behind this concept get realized only when the criteria employed is impartial and objective and far from being influenced by political or pressure factors.

The criteria are not only ineffective but are also highly impractical. Let us have a look at the criteria prescribed and the reality:

(a) Presently, creamy layer definition is limited to one generation only, i.e., to parents only. Even if the grandfather is an IAS or an industrialist, it is not considered for definition of creamy layer.

(b) Creamy layer definition is used in relation to sons/daughters only. Even if a person is an IAS, he or she is considered backward life-long. There is no time frame by which such category persons could be considered advanced.

(c) Husband's status is not considered to define advancement of a lady.

(d) Apart from few constitutional posts, none of the politicians has been included in the creamy layer. All the MPs, MLAs icluding ministers are considered backward.

(e) Almost all the Class II officers are excluded from creamy layer. Creamy layer principle is applicable only when both the father and mother of the candidate are Class II officers or either of them is promoted to Class I post before the age of 40 years.

Even if, the total emoluments of the father/mother are more than Rs. 4.5 lakhs, creamy layer principle does not apply.

(f) In defense services, only Officers equal to above the rank of Colonel are considered in the creamy layer. The officers in lower ranks very well cross the upper income limit of 2.5 lakhs. Apart from income, the other facilities provided to such officers are also not taken into consideration.

(g) Income of husband and wife is not clubbed together to define creamy layer. If both the husband and wife earn Rs. 2.40 lakhs each, creamy layer principle does not apply to their children.

(h) Income from salary and agricultural income is not clubbed together.

(i) With regard to Land holdings and ágriculture as yardstick initially persons having irrigated land equal to or more than 65% of statutory ceiling limit were included in creamy layer. Under pressure of powerful OBC and-owners, the limit was raised to 85%. In various States, the ceiling limit for irrigated land varies from 12 to 18 acres of irrigated land. Thus, practically a negligible proportion of population is covered with creamy layer definition which comprises only those people who may be equal only to the forward most of the advanced sections. Un-irrigated land, whatever may be the size, has not been considered to define creamy layer. Several States do not have upper ceiling limit. Mango, citrus, apple, and other similar plantations have been considered similar to agricultural land and same ceiling limit principle has been applied.

The annual upper income limit was Rs. 1,00,000 (one lakh) in the year 1993-94, which has been raised to Rs 2,50,000 in the year 2004. The critereia of creamy layer gets gets a sudden change in 2008 with elections to the Lok

Sabha and some state Assemblies round the corner. The government of India on 3rd Oct. 2008 raised the income ceiling for creamy layer from Rs. 2.5 lakh to Rs. 4.5 lakh annually in a move that will cover more OBCs under the reservation criteria. The Cabinet decision was communicated to the Ministry of HRD and Department of Personnel and Training (DOPT) for issuance of appropriate orders to central educational institutions and government departments for pursuance of the order.

The government however has no estimates as yet on how many people can benefit from the latest move, but some estimates suggest that close to 80 per cent of OBCs will now be eligible for affirmative action. The decision came in the wake of the Supreme Court asking the government to fill vacant seats in institutions of higher education set aside for OBCs with general category students, as these could not be filled up. *Income limit raised for creamy layer (how the creamy layer works).*

The above discussion of the criteria laid down by the Courts and the subordinate legislative's pronouncements of various yardsticks to give effect to the criteria amply makes it clear that neither the intention of the legislature nor the mind of the judiciary is clear. On the contrary it is crystal clear that the political forces in the country are far more effective in thwarting the system and process of law making. Or else it wouldn't have been possible to keep changing the upper limits of the creamy layer on and of advancing convincingly unconvincing reasons. At times one wonders whether the criteria is devised to control the unruly political forces from adversely influencing the noble concept of protective discrimination or is it the latter who invent and deploy criteria to have their way as and when required in order to meet their political hidden agenda.

A positive Law has to be objective in nature, devoid of any arbitrariness. Law should be legitimate endowed with the spirit of natural justice in consonance with rule of Law.

The framers of the constitution and successive parliaments have taken enough care and precaution to ensure that articles 15-(4) and 16(4) would only remain as exception and not become rules. Rules as it generally is seen, are exempted in the interest of justice but exemptions should never become rules so as to defeat justice. Unfortunately the trend in modern India is towards the achieving the latter at the expense of the former. This is the root of the social anomy and pertinent reason for civic strife. Unfortunately the exceptions in clauses (4) to article 15 and 16 have become almost fundamental rights in as much as the protection guaranteed against the compliance of the same is concerned. Secondly there is no state machinery evolved as yet which can monitor the effects of the protective discrimination given to backward classes and assess whether all classified target groups have taken advantage of the provision or is it only a minority that has benefited and still continue to do so not withstanding the fact that social backwardness no longer remains in its favour. In short the social and economic backwardness is often sustained or perpetrated rather than eliminated, ironically. It is also a fact that among this classified groups there is a vast majority with typical identities that have not tasted the fruits of concessions as yet.

It is unfortunate that despite decades of brain storming exercises we do not have a reasonable and acceptable criteria either for backwardness or for the so called creamy layer. The 'economic backwardness' and 'social backwardness' are made inseparable as they are considered as two sides of the same coin. Even the Constitution never sees them in isolation. Why can't economic backwardness be seen as a sole criteria as the socially 'backwards' are so because they have been economically 'backwards' for ages as a result of an unequal social structure ? This is a question that, if answered in the affirmative, would hold the key to a new social order devoid of caste and it's exploitative fall outs; for it is the *mode of production* that deprived the '*backwards*'and even the Dalits of ownership of *means of production* by one *criteria* o r the other for centuries. The 'economic backwardness' has the potential to become the most accepted criteria as all poor have the most predominant unifying factor – the hunger. Such a criteria would pull even the twice born if required while all the Dalits, and all the backwards would naturally be in descending order of the select list of beneficiaris. No wonder the Mayavati Government in up is considering even Brahmins for reservations. Let U.P, if so, hold the beacon light to enlighten all.

REFERENCES

1. Indra Sawhney vs. Union of India, A.I.R. 1993 S.C. 477 (paras 57, 58, 94a, 292, 396, 399-400).
2. Cf. Indra v. Union of India, AIR 1993 SC 477: 1992 Supp. (3) SCC 217—9-Judges; Ajay Kumar Singh v. State of Bihar, (1944) 4 SCC 401 (para 4) : 1994 (2) JT 662—Judges; Devdasan T.V. Union of India, AIR 1964 SC 179: 1964 (4 SCR 680.
3. State of A.P. v. SAgear P., (1968) 2 SCJ 778: AIR 19 68 SC 1379: 1968(3) SCR 595.
4. Preeti srivastava(Dr) v. state of M.P. (1999)7 SCC 120 (paras 13,15 and 62): AIR 1999 SC 2894.
5. Anil v. Dean Govt. Medical College, Nagpur AIR 1985 Bom. 153(para 6): Partha S.A> v. State of Mysore, AIR 1961 Mys. 220.
6. State of A.P. v. Balaram U.S.V. AIR 1972 SC 1375(1395):(1972) a SCC 660; Rajendrann C.A> v. Union of India.
7. Partap Singh v. Hardam Singh, AIR 1 UJSC 82(paras 3,6) AIR 1985 SC 1695 : (1985) 4 SCC 197;
8. See the judgements of the Supreme Court Constitution Bench in Vasanth Kumar, K.C. v. State of Karnataka, AIR 1985 SC 1495:1985 Sup. SCC 714.
9. Balaji M.R.v. State of Mysore, AIR 1963 SC 649(663): 1963Supp. (1) SCR 439; Jayasree K.S. v. State of Kerala, AIR 1976 SC 2381:(1976)3 SCC 730.
10. Chitralekha R.v. State of Mysore,AIR 1964 SC 1823 (1827): 1964 (6) SCR 368.
11. Balaji M.R.v. State of Mysore, AIR 1963 SC 649(663):1963 Supp.(1) SCR 439;

12. Rajendran P. v. State of Madras, AIR 1968 SC 1012 : 1968 (2) SCR 786.
13. State of A.P. v. BalaramU.S.V., AIR 1972 SC 1375 (1395,1399): (1972) 1 SCC 660.
14. Balaji M.R. V State of Mysore, AIR 1963 SC 649 (663) : 963 Supp. (1) SCR 439 Jayashree K.S.v. State of Kerla, AIR 1976 SC 2381 : (1976) 3 SCC 730.
15. Triloki Nath Tiku v. State of J. & K., AIR 1969 SC 1 : 1969 (1) SCR 103 : 1970 - I LLJ 629.
16. Interim Order, Ashok Kumar Thakur v. Union of India, (2007) 4 SCC 361.
17. *Ibid.,* para 2.
18. *Ibid.,* para 3.
19. *Ibid.,* para 12.
20. Indra Sawhney 1, Supra, note 3, at para 851-853.
21. *Ibid.,* para 23.
22. *Ibid.,* para 31.
23. *Ibid.,* para 32
24. *Ibid.,* paras 30-39.
25. *Ibid.,* para 40.
26. 1963 Supp (1) SCR 439 at 463.
27. (1964) 6 SCR 368 at 386-8.
28. (1968 2 SCR 786.
29. (1971) 1 SCC 38.
30. (1972) 1 SCC 660 at para 71.
31. (1973) 1 SCC 420.
32. (1975) 1 SCC 267.
33. (1976) 3 SCC 730 at 734-5.
34. (1968) 3 SCR 595.
35. DOPT, OM No. 36012/22/93-Estt. (SCT), dt. 8.9.1993 (Annexure 21.8)
36. DOPT, O.M. No. 1 36033/3/2004-Estt. (Res.) dt. 9.3.2004 (Annexure 21.8A).
37. DOPT Lr. No. 36033/5/2004-Estt. (Res.) dt. 14.10.2004. (Annexure 21.8B).

10

The Politics of Legislation and OBC Reservations

Law making in modern world is a democratic exercise, unlike the king made laws. The majority rule is just not for the majority alone. On the contrary, the government is guided by the principles of equity, justice and inclusion so as to look after the interests of minority as well. The fundamental rights and the Directive Principles of state policy in the Constitution of India are a magnificent example of a welfare state where by, the freedom, dignity and well being of a common citizen are focused and safeguarded through constitutional guarantees. However, these guarantees can not, in normal course, guarantee equality of opportunity or protection against exploitation in the absence of a viable legal frame work to enable the less privileged of the society to stand up to their relatively better placed counter parts in society (castes). Hence the need for a protective discrimination towards the under privileged classes.

The emergence of an independent India in 1947 had carried along with it the liberal democratic ethos and spirit of the British. A free India paved the way for freedom of thought and expression as a fundamental right. Universal franchise and adult suffrage in India made the opinion and choice of the people essential and indispensable for the state to have a popular government. In other words, the voice of the underprivileged and depressed sections of the society had it's say, in making legislation for the welfare of everyone in place of a few dominant sections.

The Constitution of 1950 was crystal clear that communal representation in legislatures as a form of power sharing was bad and there would be universal suffrage for all in all other seats[1]. This was a brave and significant decision -- a break from the separatist policies of the Raj. In the yea rs to come, India's Constitution was steadfast that there would be no political communal representation – even at panchayat level[2]. However, the special seats for SCs and STs in the State Legislatures and Union Parliament have been extended every 10 years since 1950.[3] After the Draft Constitution of February 1948 was published. there was some protest that the affirmative action clause for public employment should be deleted on the basis that it would promote inefficiency and place a premium on backwardness. There was also some concern that Christians and Muslims and even the SCs would be excluded from the benefits of affirmative action. Dr. B.R. Ambedkar expressed satisfaction with the test in as much as the word 'backward' was not further qualified by some adjectival limitation.[4] This did not end the controversies over affirmative action. Articles 15 and 16 became the most litigated clauses of the Indian Constitution. It is in this sense that T.T. Krishnamachari was surely right to predict that this provision would become a 'paradise for lawyers'.[5]

The major concerns of the Supreme Court were firstly that, reservations would entrench casteism for self advancement and secondly, reservations in the form of quotas could become excessive in their limits or go to those in the 'creamy layer' who would get all the benefits instead of the truly disadvantaged amongst the backward classes. The spirit of these concerns came to be reflected in the Mandal decision of 1992.[6] It made it amply clear that caste could not be the only basis for identifying backward classes, reservations should not take place in public employment in special higher posts or in promotional posts, reservations should not exceed fifty per cent and, the 'creamy layer' amongst the backward classes should be excluded from benefits.[7]

Originally OBCs were recognized as deserving beneficiaries because certain caste groups were treated as 'backward' in the Princely and other States in southern India. But who were the Other Backward Classes?[8] Various Sates defined the OBCs in their own way with an eye on the vote bank. At the level of the Union, the formal quest for an answer to this question led to the appointment of the Kaka Kalelkar Committee which reported in 1955[9] and the Bindheshwari Prasad Mandal Commission of 1979-1980[10]. The former identified about a third of India's population and the latter identified about fifty two per cent of India's population as backward. The accuracy of this estimate was itself the subject of intense debate as Mandal Commission relied up on the Census of 1931 and projected its calculations on an assumed rate of demographic growth. As a matter of fact Prime Ministers Jawaharlal Nehru, Indira Gandhi and Rajiv Gandhi were all against a reservations programme for OBCs in the Central Government. The Congress was content in extending its quota support to the SCs and STs.

The basis of identifying a 'backward' class is that it is (a) disadvantaged and, (b) discriminated against. The criterion of 'disadvantaged' is shared by not just SCs, STs and OBCs but millions of others – who do not qualify as SC, ST and OBCs. In the case of the SCs and STs, atrocities are committed against them. They are discriminated against. But this is not entirely true of the OBCs. There is little reason to equate the SCs and STs with the OBCs who are not discriminated against like the SCs and STs or disadvantaged to the extent that many other Indians who are not OBCs. That leads us to an understanding that OBC campaign is a political movement for empowerment. All poor need help. But all the same not everyone can get quota reservations. Affirmative action controversies in India are not really about helpful programmes for the disadvantaged but about quotas. For the SCs and STs, quotas may be necessary but need to be scaled down. For the OBCs, the case of quotas needs to be tested with rigor and strict scrutiny based on compelling reasons.[11]

Backward Class versus Backward caste

One of the major grievances of Backward groups was that they felt *'disempowered'.* It is worthwhile to mention the agenda of 'empowerment' behind OBC reservation as vindicated in the speech of the then Prime Minister Mr. Vishwanath Pratap Singh[12].

> *"After all, if you take the strength of the whole of the Government employees as a proportion of the population, it will be 1% or 11/2. We are under no illusion that this 1% of the population, or a fraction of it will resolve the economic problems of the whole section of 52%. No. We consciously want to give them a position in the decision-making of the country, a share in the power structure. We talk about merit. What is the merit of the system itself ? That the section which has 52% of the population gets 12.55% in Government employment."*

The historical speech of the erstwhile Prime Minister is very significant in as much as the thrust on the policy is concerned. The essential qualification or the concern happens to be social and educational backwardness which cuts across the barriers of caste and religion. But however the caste identity sneaks in to the whole scheme for the simple reason that it is impossible to assess the backwardness of an individual in India with out reference to his social identity. Hence the so called backward castes. Nevertheless it is a paradox that the expression, backward classes no longer refers or connotes class and on the contrary it has become a synonym for caste. It is remarkable that none less than the Prime Minister emphasizes the power share percentage of the Backward Castes in the power structure of the country in proportion to their numerical strength and justifies reservation. If the same logic is to be extended to ridiculous lengths, then each caste needs to be given a proportionate share in the power structure, no matter what ever its economic and social status is. Nothing can be more terrifying than such a visualization. It leads us to a situation where in there is neither a class legislation nor is there a classified legislation. It all appears to be a caste legislation which the framers of the constitution had never intended. This, indeed, is a *fait accompli* that leaves the expression "secular" in the preamble of the constitution at cross roads.

Although OBCs have been recipients of reservations both before and after Independence, the Mandal Commission Report of 1980 recommended a huge proliferation of OBC groups to around 3,000 and more, covering some 52 per cent of the population for whom the Mandal Report recommended a reservation quota of 27 per cent generally. The recommendations were of course not unjustified in principal. This report was resurrected in 1990 by the V.P. Singh Government provoking riots. The Supreme Court's decision is popularly known as the Mandal case (1992) evolved a compromise to reconcile the claims of the disadvantaged and the meritorious and gave a detailed judgment on many issues. This precipitated a showdown between the Supreme Court and Parliament whereby the latter amended the Constitution several times to override and overrule the Supreme Court.

Since the implementation of the Mandal Commission Report, political parties of various lines were indeed compelled to give the party a backward caste friendly appearance. At the same time Many political parties tried to perform a fine balancing act to retain its hold on upper castes and also to make some gains over the backward castes.

The Cold War in Qouta Politics

V.P. Singh announced the implementation the Mandal Commission Report on August 7, 1990 to silence some of his bitter critics in his party as well as his allies. He thought that it would enable him to create a powerful dent into the vote bank of BJP by slicing it into two units the forward and backward caste, the latter's support which he could also lay claim to[13]. Caste violence suddenly acquired a national character. The movement resulted in hooliganism and vandalism and almost degenerated into a street affair and threw the anti-reservation stir in disarray and confusion. The final verdict of the Supreme Court ordering the exclusion of creamy layer, which in other words was tantamount to acceptance of an economic criteria, gained greater legitimacy and acceptance for parties like Congress, BJP and the Left who had earlier demanded the inclusion of an economic criterion.

The announcement of implementation of the Mandal Report caused a great deal of consternation in the BJP camp[14]. The BJP feared that it would cause a severe erosion of their vote banks by depriving them of OBC votes and inflicting a schism within the Hindu religion itself. Severe condemnation was the initial reaction to the announcement[15]. Later the party retracted its statements fearing the antagonizing of BCs[16].

The Left parties like Communist Party of India (CPI) and the Communist Party of India (Marxist) (CPM)[17] were always in favour of reservation policy for the backward classes. While the CPI is for total implementation of the report without the economic criterion for ten years CPI(M) is for the criterion of economic criterion. Both these parties are of the firm opinion that reservation in jobs alone will not improve the conditions of the BCs. Land reforms and economic policy changes should also be effected to improve the lot of the BCs. It is surprising as to how the Left reconciled the backward class quota with the *'class war' and 'class less society'*.

The Mandal Impact on State Politics

Political parties took almost a different approach to suit the situation prevalent in various states. Uttar Pradesh, with its huge BC and being the state where the disputed site of Ram Mandir is located, was seriously affected by both the Mandal and Mandir issue. Mulayam Singh Yadav's decision to implement 27% reservation for OBCs disturbed the entire social fabric in the state. His decision would have resulted in an increase of more than fifty per cent in reservations. But he justified his decision by stating that several states in the south like Tamil Nadu and Karnataka were pursuing reservation policies which exceeded the Fifty per cent limit. The BJP and Congress (I) demanded the introduction of and economic criterion which was stoutly opposed by Mulayam Singh Yadav fearing the alienation of his castes. Muslims were also beneficiaries according to the report, and Mulayam Singh's appeasement of Muslims served the BJP well to incite communal passions[18]. The Mandir issue overwhelmed the Mandal issue so much so that the casteist issue got gradually erased from the minds of the backwards. The 1993 assembly elections saw the emergence of (Bahujan Samaj Party) BSP as a major factor in UP elections. Realising the potential of Dalit-Muslim-Backward Class alliance Mulayam Singh Yadav began efforts towards this purpose in right earnest. Thus the alliance contributed significantly to the victory of BSP-SJP combine under the leadership of Kanshi Ram and Mulayam Singh Yadav.

Laloo Prasad Yadav in imitation of V.P. Singh overhauled the entire reservation formula adopted in Bihar by doing away with two unique and widely accepted provisions. He annulled the provisions providing reservations for the economically weaker sections among the forward castes. The provision, which prevented the affluent among BC from taking advantage of the reservation scheme, was removed. Laloo justified his move to remove the economic criterion saying that the Supreme Court does not allow the inclusion of economic criterion in identifying backwardness.[19]

The Congress began to make valiant attempts to infiltrate the powerful backward class vote bank deftly carved out by Laloo Prasad Yadav. In order to woo OBCs Congress gave only 9.3% of the tickets of the Lok Sabha elections to Yadavas while 16.6% were given to the non-Yadavas. BJP too attempted to wean away some of the Yadavas from Laloo Prasad Yadavs sphere of influence. L.K. Advani thought of winning away the masses by his "Rath Yatra". Laloo Yadav issued orders of arrest of L.K. Advani on October 23, 1991. Laloo's strategy paid him handsomely at the Lok Sabha elections in 1991 when he maintained his position slightly lesser than in 1989 (i.e. from 30 to 28). At the same time the BJP and Congress were the major losers with their tally being reduced from 9 seats in 1989 to 5 and from 4 seats in 1989 to 1 in 1991.

The Congress (I) in M.P decided to capitalize on the political consciousness among the OBCs[20] by demanding the implementation of the Mahajan commission Report which had recommended a reservation of 35% for Backward classes. The congress (I)'s appeal was a blow to the BJP which had opposed the Mahajan Commission Report[21]. A hot contest between the Congress (I) and BJP ensued in nominating the largest number of OBC candidates. However as the election results of 1993 revealed, the strength of BJP MLAs from the lower castes declined but at the same time increased from the upper castes. The election results of 1993 made it apparent to the BJP that its steps to cultivate the OBC is inadequate towards shedding its upper caste image. They decided to bring about a characteristic change in the rank and file of its organization by conceding several key posts in the party structure to OBC and SC/ST[22]. This incensed its major feeder organization the Rashtriya Swayam Sevak Sahgh (RSS) which felt that the BJP is dithering from its main ideological plank i.e., casteless society or Hindu unity[23].

In Karnataka in 1986 the Ramakrishna Hegde provided for 68 per cent reservation which covered 92 per cent of the population including the socially and politically powerful Lingayats and Vokkaligas. Chinnappa Reddy

Commission had recommended the scaling down of OBC reservations from the existing 50 per cent to 38 per cent. Veerappa Moily government implemented a diluted version of the Chinnappa Reddy Commission report amounting to the total reservation being increased to 73 per cent (23 per cent for SC and ST and 50 per cent for OBCs). This move was resorted to by Moily in a bid to appease a few communities as only a month lay ahead for the Zilla Parishad and Taluk committee elections and also only four months lay ahead for the assembly elections. Vokkaligas and Lingayats whom the commission had requested to be excluded from the BC list were accommodated by creating a fourth category of BCs. The decision of Supreme Court prevented him not only from increasing the reservation quota but also resulted in decreasing the prevalent 68 per cent reservation to 50 per cent. Dissidence within the party combined with failure on the reservation front inflicted a crushing defeat in the 1994 Assembly polls in Karnataka.

Almost all political parties in all States have assumed a Backward Caste *messiah role* ever since the Mandal movement has officially been justified by it's implementation. The constraints of space refrain me from giving a detailed account of political developments across the length and breadth of the country over the issue. However it is no secret for it is still hot with increasing demand for 'inclusion' 'expansion' and 'equity'. In Rajasthan we have recently observed the political power of the gujjars that shook the foundations of State. Despite the efforts of BJP to appease the belligerent groups assuring their inclusion in OBC, it had to face disastrous defeat in 2009 assembly polls.

The concept of creamy layer introduced through *Indra sahani* case is a very important yardstick designed to ensure justice for those stake holders with in the OBC who are not the cream. In a way it is measuring rod to protect the backwards from with in. An expert committee to concretise the 'creamy layer' and their exclusion was created. It submitted a report in March 1993. The court's observation stated— "the correct criterion for judging the forwardness of the forwards among the backward classes is to measure their capacity not in terms of the capacity of others in their class, but in terms of the capacity of the members of the forward classes. If they cross the 'line' of backwardness, they should be taken out from the backward classes and should be made disentitled to the provision meant for the said classes". This is pertinent to understand the concept of the 'creamy layer'. The exclusion of the 'creamy layer' constitutes actually an important complement to the principle which integrates holistically all sections of the OBC and the non-OBC poor. It is this unity which will sustain the struggle to eliminate the existing social and economic inequality.

However the aim and purpose behind this concept get realized only when the criteria employed is impartial and objective and far from being influenced by political or pressure factors. Unfortunately the facts are contrary to it as political considerations creep in. The critereia of creamy layer gets a sudden change in 2008 with elections to the Lok Sabha and some State Assemblies round the corner. The government of India on 3rd Oct. 2008 raised the income ceiling for creamy layer from Rs. 2.5 lakh to Rs. 4.5 lakh annually in a move that will cover more OBCs under the reservation criteria. The Cabinet decision was communicated to the Ministry of HRD and Department of Personnel and Training (DOPT) for Issuance of appropriate orders to central educational institutions and government departments for pursuance of the order.

"The Union Cabinet today gave its approval for revising the income criteria for creamy layer from the present Rs. 2.5 lakh per annum to Rs. 4.5 lakh per annum," Information and Broadcasting Minister Priyaranjan Dasmunshi[24] said.

Conclusion

The law making process with regard to framing of a Reservation Policy in India for OBCs has been adversely influenced by politics of appeasement. Political parties with no exception have always tried to sit on the fence when it did not clearly ensured the political prospects. The sooner they estimated the gain they wasted no time in orchestrating for reservation in favor of a cast or a community. It is understandable that in a democracy political parties need support of certain vote banks to ensure their existence in the legislative bodies. But the tragedy is that the ideals of democracy and the spirit of the constitution in as much as equality and secularism is concerned have been compromised. Caste has remained and continues to remain as dominant factor determining politics of India though the framers of the constitution had only tried to remove the negative impact of Caste by making special provisions to articles 14,15 and 16. It is sad that today the exceptions have become rules. The law making is a secular process. It is high time that the political parties have realized that caste is the basic divisive factor of the Indian society and any adherence to it would only further disintegrate the society and the country. Absence of such a realization would only render the Constitution a piece of historical interest.

REFERENCES

1. Debates in VIII CAD 313-355 (26 May 1949), particularly the speech of Sir Tajamul Hussain, VIII CAD 332-338 (26 May 1949).
2. *Ibid.*
3. Article 334 of the Constitution of India, as amended (Sixty Second and Seventy Ninth).
4. *Ibid.*
5. Article 334 of the Constitution of India, as amended (Sixty Second and Seventy Ninth).
6. VII CAD at 695-699; and the reply of B.R. Ambedkar at 700-702.
7. T.T. Krishna machari, VII CAD 699 (30 November 1948) and B.R. Ambedkar, VII CAD 700 (30 November 1948).
8. Indra Sawhney 1992 Supp (3) SCC 217.
9. Indra Sawhney 1992 Supp (3) SCC 217.

10. Marc Galanter, "Who are the Other Backward Classes: An Introduction to a Constitutional Puzzle", in 13 Economic and Political Weekly 1812 (1978).
11. Report of the (First) Backward Classes Commission (30 March 1955), under the chairmanship of Shri Kaka Kalelkar. Its Report was rejected in 1961.
12. Report of the Second Backward Classes Commission (31 December 1980), Chaired by B.P. Mandal.
13. See, M. Nagaraj v. Union of India (2006) 8 SCC 212.
14. Reservation for Backward Classes. Mandal Commission Report.1980, Introduction, Aklank Publ. Delhi
15. Patriot: New Delhi 26.12.1990.
16. Reddy, Muralidhar R., 1990: Where is the Consensus? Interview with K.L. Sharma, BJP General Secretary, September 29 October 12, p. 29.
17. (Ibid: 15).
18. Reddy, Muralidhar R., 1990: Political Ploys: Frontline, September 29-October 12, 1990, pp. 21, 26, 27, 31, 32.
19. Reddy, Muralidhar R., 1990: Political Ploys: Frontline, September 29-October 12, 1990, pp. 21, 26, 27, 31, 32.
20. Hassan, Zoya, 1998: Quest for Power: Oppositional Movements and Post Congress Policies in Uttar Pradesh, New Delhi: OUP: pp: 102, 103, 131-132.
21. Chaudhary, Kameshwar, 1993: New Reservation Policy: EPW, June 5 pp. 1145-47.
22. National Mail 19 November, 1993.
23. Hindustan Times, 4 November, 1993.
24. National Mail, 16 December 1993
25. The Hindutva life force works in the cause of our society" organizer 19 December 1993 p. 17 and 5 December, 1995 p. 7.
26. Press Trust of India / New Delhi October 3, 2008, 19:02 IST.

11
Gender Budget and Women Education

Women historically have never been given the required importance vis a vis man in the entire world, be it in the field of politics or economy not to mention education. History is full with stories of exploitation, humiliation and suppression of women across the world. It will be surprising to know that even England, which is known as the 'mother' of parliaments, has enacted equal voting rights through universal franchise for women only in the first quarter of the 20th century. The subject of women empowerment or women's liberation is so vast that it would take volumes to touch up on each area of concern in this regard. Literacy, equal rights, emancipation from bondage, empowerment are some of the areas of focus for women's advancement in society. However, what is more important for a true empowerment of women is her equal participation in a mode of production, i.e., the *economy*. This is one area which has not been given required importance at least in India. A casual look at the statistics of women manual labourers and construction workers reflects a pathetic position of women in India.

I am reminded of Nargis in the movie *'Mother India'* who struggles through out her life to make a living and to raise her kids without a living husband. The story is not different even in modern India offer more than 60 years of independence. Women can never be liberated in the absence of a system of education which gives her an equal opportunity to make her best and realize her ambitions. The common image of women as a 'dependent' on the charity of man and society with *kicks* and *kisses* syndrome is the most unfortunate thing to prevail in the country. Unlike in the West, women in India are euphemistically protected while at the same time, they are exploited in one form or the other. What a women requires is not protection but promotion; an encouragement to participate along with men in various economic activities of society. It is only when a women is educationally equal, she is socially and politically equal to men. Because, to quote Karl Marx *'the consciousness of an individual is determined by his social existence'*[1].

The Law is in favour

The most revolutionary development happened in India is the enactment of the Hindu Succession Act 1956 and the Hindu Marriage Act 1955.These two acts have recognized the status of a women for the first time in India as equal to that of man. For the first ever time, the provision of divorce was made in law and equally the consent of a women for a marriage, besides qualifying age, were made compulsory. The Hindu Succession Act recognizes the right to property to a women as opposed to the ancient schools of thought the Mitakshara and Dayabhaga. The Indian Succession Act of 1925 was equally a progressive legislation recognizing the importance of women in matters of property. Over the years the law in India, has been so improved to provide equal status to women in all fields. Chapter 3 of the Constitution through article 15(3) makes special provisions for women and children. In short, the conditions required for an equal development of women in India do exist at least in law. The question is what is that which is enslaving the women in India still ? It is surely the educational backwardness.

Reservations about *Reservation*

The answer and the reason for the above question is not far to seek. The epithet given by Shakespeare, "frailty thy name is women" seems to be still relevant in Indian context. The policy makers though make provisions in law for empowerment of women, they fail to translate the same into action more often than not. Ever since the first amendment to the Constitution took place in 1951 (article *15(4)) the State was only concerned with special class of citizens known as SC, ST or OBCs. Women were never treated as a special class. It is irony that social and educational backwardness being the reason to treat people as special class women in India in spite of being socially educationally backward, they were never given reservations in jobs in the country except in few states like Chhattisgarh. How can a girl or women, being dependent on either father or husband for her basic survival without a formal qualification or skill to seek employment, be liberated in true sense of this term ? This is a million dollar question. Conversely, it is evident in the society that women who are economically independent either by way of an employment or some property to their name or through an independent source of income, have often exhibited great courage even to an extent of separating from their oppressive husbands. In short economic security for women is sine-qua-non for her empowerment which is only possible through educational empowerment which eventually leads to her liberation. The next important question is whether the govt. followed the policy of Gender budgeting –a trend of the 20th century with regard to Education- especially the higher.

Gender Budgeting

Gender Budgeting is the trend of the day. Across the world, the importance of women in development is acknowledged by way of substantial allocations in favour of all round empowerment of women. Gender Budgeting is an ongoing process which helps to look at General Budgets from a Gender Perspective. It is an exercise to translate stated gender commitments of the government into budgetary commitments. Gender Budgeting is, in simple terms, allocation of resources exclusively for women oriented programmes or the proportionate share of women development in all programmes.

How serious is India in so far as women's empowerment is concerned is a question never answered satisfactorily. Let us have look at the priorities of budget in favour of women in the planned development scheme of the country;

FIVE YEAR PLANS AND THE SHARE OF WOMEN[2]

S. No.	*Five Year Plans*	*Views on Women*
1.	First Plan (1951-56)	Sets up the central social welfare board in 1953 to promote women welfare work through voluntary organizations, charitable trusts etc.
2.	Second Plan (1956-61	supported the development of mahila mandals to work at the grassroots.
3.	Third, Fourth and interim plan (1961-74)	Had provisions for **women's education**, pre-natal and child health services, supplementary feeding for children, nursing and expectant.
4.	Fifth Plan (1974-78)	A major shift in the approach towards women from welfare to development.
5.	Sixth Plan (1980-1985)	Accepted Women's development as a separate Economic agenda. Took a multidisciplinary approach with a three-pronged thrust on health, **education and employment**.

S. No.	*Five Year Plans*	*Views on Women*
6.	Seventh Plan (1985-90)	Had the objective of bringing women into the mainstream of national development.
7.	Eighth Plan (1992-97)	Saw a paradigm shift from development to empowerment and benefits to women in the core sector of education, health and employment. Outlay for women rose from Rs. 4 crore in the First Plan to Rs. 2,000 crore in the Eight Plan.
8.	Ninth Plan (1997-02	Had Empowerment of women as its strategic objective. Accepted the concept of a women's component plan to assure that at least 30% of funds/ benefits from all development sector flow to women.
9.	Tenth Plan (2002-07)	Suggests specific strategies, policies and programs for the empowerment of women.
10.	Eleventh Plan (2007-11)	Special measures for gender empowerment and equity will be an essential component of the 11th Plan. The Plan will have a special focus on four aspects-violence against women (VAW), economic empowerment, political participation and women's health.

These areas of thrust in the successive plans are any thing but focussed programme for exclusive educational empowerment of women.

The Commonwealth Secretariat GRB (Gender Related budget) initiative identified possible indicators that could be used to prepare a GRB statement. These indicators are proposed as starting points for a continuous process of monitoring resource allocations and linking these to government commitments and policies. They include:

1. Share of total expenditure targeted to gender equality programmes.
2. Gender balance in public sector employment which looks at the number of women and men at different levels and in different jobs.
3. Share of expenditures devoted to women's priority needs from public services.
4. Share of expenditure devoted to national women's machinery and to the gender units within each ministry.
5. Share of expenditure devoted to women's priority income transfer which would include child support grants that provide monthly payments to care givers of young children in poor households.
6. Gender balance in business support such as subsidies, training or credit provided by the Ministries of trade and Industry and Agriculture.
7. Gender balance in public sector contracts including contracts awarded, including contracts to build homes for public works.
8. Gender balance in decision making bodies, forums and committees.
9. Gender balance in government training programmes.

The Commitments of Planning Commission

Let us briefly refresh ourselves with the Plan related priorities that were placed in the last five Plans with regard to the women empowerment through Education.

7th FYP (1985-1990)

Introduced monitoring of *27 major women specific schemes* and quantum of funds flowing to women by DWCD, Mo HRD.

8th FYP (1992-1997)

For the first time highlighted the need for general *Development Programmes* to reflect *greater gender sensitivity.*

9th FYP (1997-2002)

Adopted **Women's Component Plan'** ensuring that *'not less than **30%** of funds/benefits be earmarked in all women related sectors'.*

10th FYP (2002-2007)

Sought to tie up concepts of WCP and GB to play complementary role to each other.

11th Plan (2007-12)

It states that –*'gender equity requires adequate provisions to be made in policies and schemes across Ministries and Departments. It also entails strict adherence to gender budgeting across the board.'*

The ministry of Women and Child Development, government of India, has been laying emphasis on Gender Budgeting and sensitizing all decision makers in this regard. Series of orientation courses and training programmes across the length and breadth of the country towards this end. Gender Budgeting is as good as the special allotments made in favour of scheduled castes and scheduled tribes in the country which is otherwise known as tribal sub-plan (TSP) and special component plant (SCP). The Planning Commission in India is committed to the Gender Budgeting as well and implored upon the streets to adhere to the norms of the same. In TSP and SCP, the governments are supposed to spend the allocations exclusively for the upliftment of scheduled castes and tribes. Any deviation is viewed seriously by the Accountant General of a state and the CAG of India. However, no such seriousness is seen with regard to gender budgeting as yet in any field of development.

The following table shows the poor progress of Gender Budget in various ministries in GOI[3]:

Year	*No. of Ministries (No. of Demands)*	*Total Magnitude of Gender Budget (BE) (in Rs. crore)*
2005-06	9 (10)	14378.68 **(2.79 %)**
2006-07	18 (24)	28736.53 **(5.09%)**
2007-08	27 (33)	31177.96 **(4.5%)**
2008-09	27 (33)	27661.67 **(3.68%)**
2009-10	27 (33)	56857.61 **(5.57%)**
2010 -11	**28 (33)**	**67749.80 (6.11%)**

There seems to be an erratic trend in the allocation of resources towards women related development programmes till now. It is high time that the governments in the states and in the centre vow to strictly implement the gender budgeting norms so that the economic well-being of women is guaranteed by way of proper infra-structure which in turn heavily depends up on literacy and more so on higher Education.

It is great sigh of relief that women have been given a statutory reservation of upto 50% in PRIs and Local Bodies to contest the elections. Chhattisgarh is one state, where 50% reservations in PRIs is provided. The result is magnificently encouraging. Though it is a fact that the husbands run the show on behalf of their wives, yet the wives are put forward willingly-unwillingly and are recognised as politically important. This is a good beginning from the bad ending in the history. Similarly, women need reservation in economic activities such as provision of licences, establishment of industries or participation in bidding for state-run activities and supplies. The encouragement of women in these areas of activity connected with state will surely usher in an era of economic independence for women for, women would be indispensable if the above activities are to be obtained to one's advantage. This would enhance the position of women even in most orthodox families. It is a slow but steady progress towards economic independence of women. But what is more essential is empowering the women educationally with a view to enable them to avail the opportunities of. And this education can mean nothing if it does not consist of higher learning in under graduate and post graduate courses.

The Discouraging Picture of Women Literacy

The government has expressed a strong commitment towards education for all, however, India still has one of the lowest female literacy rates in Asia. In 1991, less than 40 percent of the 330 million women aged 7 and over were literate, which means today, there are over 200 million illiterate women in India. While the GER continues to be low for the overall population, there are large variations among the various categories of population based on gender, urban or rural habitation and reach and poor. Below Table illustrates these divergences.

Enrolment Ratio under Different groups of Population[4]

The above table reveals that as per the survey conducted by different organizations, the enrolment ratio has been different in relation to social background and sex; the latter seems to be more important in comparison. As per 2001 census, the GER in males was 17.1% whereas, it was just

	GER			NER	EER
Source/Year	**SES 2006-07**	**Census 2001**	**NSS 2003**	**NSS 2003**	**NSS 2003**
All	9.7	13.8	13.2	13.2	59.0
Gender					
Male	11.1	17.1	15.3	12.3	62.9
Female	7.9	10.2	11.0	8.7	54.1
Caste					
Schedule Tribes	4.6	7.5	5.0	4.0	57.4
Schedule Castes	7.0	8.4	7.5	5.9	56.4
OBC			11.34		
Others			24.89		
Religion					
Hindu			12.0	9.0	57.0
Muslim			8.2	6.3	58.1
OtherReligion			30.9	24.3	65.8
Rural		9.0	7.8	6.1	51.5
Urban		24.5	27.2	21.9	66.0
Poor			2.43		
Non-Poor			12.81		

10.2% in case of women. As per NSS, in 2003, the GER for males was 15.3% whereas for females it was just 11%. The data in the table depicts social factors such as caste, tribe, urban-rural or religion to cast a difference in enrolment ratio. However, the difference between male : female ratio appears to be proportionately affected. It is a fact that the Government of India in its National Policy on Education, has updated in 1992, and the 1992 programme of action reaffirmed the government's commitment to increase the literacy levels in women especially by providing special attention to girls and scheduled castes and scheduled tribes. In 1970s as per the data of Registrar General and Census Commissioner, India, only 22% of women were literate. The scenario seems to be improved in 1991 when 39% of women were recorded as literates. We can say, there has been a heartening development so far as women's literacy is concerned in two decades between 1970 - 1990. For the entire country, we saw a decrease in the gender gap in literacy from 1980 onwards. Still the disparity between the sexes in terms of literacy has been on the rise in few states of the country. In 1991, the female literacy rate in urban areas was recorded as more than that of rural areas viz., 64% and 34% respectively[5]. Despite a substantial increase in literacy rates, both in urban and rural areas, the gender gap has not seemed to have decreased.

Besides the ever increasing gap of gender in urban-rural divide aspect, the enrolment ratio of women has been discouragingly uneven from state to state in the country in the last few decades. As per the 1991 census, Kerala stands out as the state for highest women literacy rate with over 86%, Mizoram as second with 79% of women literates. The unpleasant side of the story happens to be in Bihar and Uttar Pradesh with just 30% of women literates. Incidentally, these two are the most populous states in the country. It is also observed that the literacy levels in women have a high co-relation with health indicators of population. For instance, Kerala has the lowest IMR with highest life expectancy whereas, Bihar and Uttar Pradesh have lowest life expectancies[6]. In Rajasthan, Women Literacy Rate has been appalling with just 12% of women being literates. States such as Gujarat, Sikkim, West Bengal, Meghalaya, Karnataka, Assam, Haryana, Odisha, Madhya Pradesh, Andhra Pradesh etc. have been oscillating in female literacy rates from 40 – 50%. In terms of enrolment in schools, in most of the states, more than half of the girls aged between 6 – 14 were reported to be attending school. Though Bihar has the lowest enrolment for both girls and boys, still happens to be a larger gender gap with only 38% in comparison to 64% of boys[7]. In terms of drop-out rates, it is estimated that 45% of the girls stop going to school between grades I to V, whereas, in case of boys, it is only 45%[8]. As per the IIPS 1995 Report, in early 90s, only 55% of girls between 11 – 14 age group were attending school whereas it was 61% for the ages below 11 years. This shows that with increase in age, there seems to be decrease in attendance to school. Factors such as poverty, honour syndrome, caste related, cultural practices could be a reason for such a decrease in enrolment ratio.

Education for Empowerment of Women

It goes without saying that women cannot be liberated without being imparted formal education atleast for 5-6 years. The necessity is more in a strictly gender biased society such as India[9]. Unfortunately in India, around, 59% women have only a primary level of education which is surely insufficient to liberate themselves from the clutches of orthodox tradition and to empower themselves to stand-up to the challenges of modern society. In the field of higher education, it is observed that the enrolment is extremely limited below 10% of the age-group between 18 – 23. Even in this, women account only for one-third of the students in colleges and universities[10]. The imbalance in the sex-ratio in higher education is evident except in faculties such as engineering and commerce and, the faculty of education, as it seems to be the natural choice for women.

Some of the reasons for a disproportionate rate of literacy in women and poor enrolment in higher education could be as under :

(a) Indian society being mostly male dominated, the very idea of equating a woman with a man is still not so saleable an idea, at least, in rural India and as a result though in principle, female literacy is accepted but somewhere on the way, it is infected by Drop Out syndrome.

(b) Poverty, unemployment are strong economic disadvantages which affect people living below poverty line. As a consequence, the parents find it hard to send children especially girls to schools, as it is no less expensive an affair.

(c) Social factors such as caste, religion, discrimination of sexes, takes its own toll in terms of women literacy.

Infrastructural facilities are yet to be provided in full-fledged fashion so that parents are encouraged. Lack of pecca buildings, roads, drinking water etc have a discouraging effect. In Uttarpradesh 53% of schools did not have water supply while 80% did not have latrines[11].

(d) The relatively poor enrolment ratio of girls in higher education seems to be related to cultural factors such as early marriages of girls and suppressive gender value systems.

(e) Lack of infrastructure such as hostels, exclusive women colleges in adequate number, women teachers and gender friendly transport systems appear to discourage women's participation in higher education.

The above reasons are only illustrative. What is more important is participation of women in the field of higher education as the primary or middle class levels cannot truly educate them towards achieving equality, freedom and economic independence. Though successive governments through successive five-year plans avowedly exhibited commitment towards women literacy, the outcome does not appear to be satisfactory. Somewhere, lack of will or determination on the part of the government surfaces in terms of women empowerment. The gender budgeting is an area which needs to be sincerely given thrust and emphasis. Provision of allocations could be made on equal basis and with exclusive focus with regard to education of women particularly in colleges and universities. Some of the areas of focus could be the following :

(a) Proportionate number of hostels in colleges, universities and other institutions of higher learning must be provided to reach out to rural women students.

(b) Exclusive women's colleges and universities or institutions need to be sanctioned to make way for a free and secure educational environment for women to bring out their inherent talents and capacities.

(c) Exclusive means of transportation for women students and faculty could be budgeted to ensure personal safety and tension free academic pursuits.

(d) Sufficient financial allocations may be earmarked to create on-campus placement facilities for women aspirants.

(e) Academic infrastructure such as libraries, laboratories etc. need to be created for pursuing higher levels of learning.

(f) Scholarship schemes and fellowship programmes may be specially implemented for women from weaker sections or from backward areas.

Special Audit

Tribal sub-plan for development of scheduled tribes and special component plan for the benefit of scheduled castes has been in implementation for the last few decades and the Accountant General conducts complete audit of the allotment and allocations made under these two schemes to keep a vigil on the purpose of expenditure. Similarly there is a need for exclusive accountability of the authorities concerned with the execution of gender budgeted schemes and programmes. It is only then, that the objective behind the gender budget is fulfilled. The government must see to it that in the sector of higher learning, adequate resources are allocated for women's education and equally it must ensure that the same is expended as per the norms laid down, or else, it would be a futile exercise to earmark funds just in the name of gender budgeting.

The Government of India from the year 2002 has been emphatically insisting upon implementation of gender budgeting in almost all departments of development. The Department of Women and Child Development has been nodal department to monitor the gender budget related aspects in all the departments and look after the needs of women empowerment accordingly. The higher education departments in almost all states today, do not seem to have adhered to the norms of the gender budgeting. It is high time that the government made a serious effort towards streamlining the administrative channels and meant business strictly. A lack-lustre attitude of government towards an important area of gender budgeting in higher budgeting could only mean half-hearted disposition towards women's empowerment, be it economical or educational.

Implementing Gender Budget in Higher Education

Gender Budgeting in Higher Education will create a sea change in the economic and political fields of women development. The required infrastructure for mobility of women will be created when special allocations are made in Center and State budgets. Following ways and means can be really productive in imlimenting and monitoring of Gender budgeting in Higher Education;

(a) Accountability of the State implementing Agencies and Authorities is pin pointedly determined in the event of diversion of resources.

(b) As against prevailing system of general pool of financial grants where any thing can be done in the name of HRD a tailor made earmarking of resources will only be utilised for areas of women's Colleges, Universities, Hostels, Labs, and related infrastructure.

(c) It is also essential that these financial allocations are placed in a high power Committee headed by qualified women with maximum number of women academicians and Bureaucrats as members.

(d) Periodic review of schemes and their execution can be taken up by the Committee and recommendations can be made in terms of quality and control.

(e) We need an apex body at national levels to advice the Planning Commission of India and the Ministry of HRD. All State Governments can follow suit and come up with their own Bodies towards this objective. (It is worth mentioning here that there are similar agencies and Bodies in matters of Minority or SC and STs. After all, the Constitution of India specially lays down in Art.15(3) provisions for the welfare of women and children.)

(f) This calls for a legislation or rule making exercise by the Subordinate Legislation, what ever it takes for that matter, to clearly spell out the rules of the game.

(g) Sensitizing various partner or line Departments in the process is equally important task to be accomplished for various budgetary allocations from various Departments are dovetailed to the budget of Higher Educaion such as Tribal Welfare Department for Head 41, and Scheduled Caste Development Department for Head 69, Special Component Plan etc.

(h) The State Planning Commissions must review the Gender Budget programmes periodically with the Dept. of Higher Education and other related Departments.

(i) The University Grants Commission has pivotal role to play with regard to allocations to Universities across the country. The Comptroller and Auditor General of India and the Accountant Generals of States have their respective roles to play in overseeing the expenditure of the gender budgeted items.

(j) The Publics Accounts Committees of State Legislative Assemblies and that of Parliament have an imperative duty caste up on them to take to task any Public Servant and the Govt. for violations. These are some illustrative strategic ways and means to achieve the purpose of gender budget and are not exhaustive.

Gender budgeting in Higher Education sector will have long term impact on the economic empowerment of women in the country in terms of capacity development. Besides women's representation in services sector, development of entrepreneurship will be a major out come. Women with formal qualifications in Management, Accountancy or other self employment courses can be involved in income generating activities and enterprises. There are immense possibilities which can be explored by the Government Departments to facilitate women towards this goal.

Encouraging Women SHGs

Apart from job reservations, women need to be given a sufficient importance and a role to play in the general economy of the country by way of encouraging women entrepreneurship. It is heartening to note that in Chhattisgarh, there are more than 70,000 self-help groups of women. However, majority of them are not engaged in economic activity for want of wherewithal. Adequate financial resources are required to be pumped in to activate these SHGs for a sustained economic activity. There are many trades associated with daily provisions of society which can be handled by women. The government needs to make special provisions to encourage the same.

Women can Lead Agriculture

Agriculture is one area which is not included in public sector even today. With vast chunks of un-cultivable land available in the country it is high time that the state seriously contemplated bringing agriculture into public sector. The focus could be on women participation in agriculture as majority of women are in the rural areas and are identified with agriculture-related labour activities. This would arrest the unhealthy trend of migration of forced women labour to cities mostly engaged in construction activities often resulting in exploitation.. Similarly allied activities such as dairy, poultry and minor forest produce related trades (for instance bidi manufacturing) can be developed exclusively in the domain of gender budgeting with a view to strengthen women Self Help Groups. The Amul's white revolution is a spectacular example of women's economic empowerment in the country. Similar exercises can be replicated elsewhere in the country.

Media's Positive Role

The media has a more positive role in this regard than the harm it is doing today to the concept of women liberation. A saga of family drama is often telecast in various channels mostly belittling the stature of a woman and glorifying her slavery into male chauvinistic idioms of faithfulness and family bond. Roles of women are depicted as subservient to that of men. Countless advertisements project women as objects of sensual appeal or sometimes utterly stupid femme fettle The media needs to be serious towards women empowerment and project the ideal picture of future woman of the country who would be independent self-reliant and equal to man as it is the reality in the West. The state should enact stringent laws against the outrage of women and their modesty in the media.

NGOs to Spearhead the Movement

The spirited social groups and NGOs have an important role in supporting the cause of economic empowerment of women. Mostly these organizations are engaged in battle against suppression and exploitation of women which is a noble cause. However, they can play a more pro-active role towards economic independence of women by way of taking up individual or group issues of women's economic activities and fight for required relief. Gender inequalities are an important cause for economic inequalities as opined by Amartya Sen in his famour nobel winning book 'Freedom as Development'. It is responsibility of all parents also to practise gender budgeting within the home. After all *charity begins at home.* It is only by a concerted efforts and a united struggle that women liberation can be truly achieved. The beginning in this marathon is surely literacy but most importantly, it is the economic self-reliance that truly liberates woman from the shackles of exploitation and suffering. Let's not forget that *"the hand that rocks the cradle rules the world."*

The following table reflects the position of encouragement to women by the government in India over the years.

Conclusion

It is high time that the State has taken the call and seriously thought about the need for a gender budget in Higher Education field. After all, it is higher learning that can only emancipate a woman from the shackles of oppression and exploitation. The plethora of schemes announced from time to time by the Dept. of Women and Child Development for the development of women and their empowerment will end up in fiasco in the absence of exclusive budget for women education. University Grants Commission must bear the torch and lead the campaign in all sincerity. The community of academicians and intellectuals should rise to the occasion and sensitize the policy makers. Let us not forget that there is good lot of Advisors (intellectuals from NGOs) in the Planning Commission of India who can blow the whistle. Media has also can be a substantial contributor in this mission by highlighting areas of concern. The National Women's Commission cannot afford to remain a silent spectator in the midst of pathetic scenario of woman education in the country. It has the statutory obligation to fight for the cause of women such as the one we are discussing till now.

REFERENCES

1. See *Karl Marx, Economic and Political Manuscripts 1848,*
2. "Women's Empowerment Dimensions and Directions" Social Welfare, March 2009.
3. Source NPCCD New Delhi.
4. Chairman UGC's Nehru Memorial Lecture, University of Mumbai, Nov. 24, 2006.
5. Registrar General and Census Commissioner, 1993.
6. India Registrar General 1996 : IRG 1995.
7. International Institute for Population Sciences 1995. India National Family Health Survey 1992-93, Bombay.
8. The World Bank 1997a, India Achievement and Challenges in Reducing Poverty, Washington DC.
9. Jeffrey, Roger and Alaka M. Basu eds, 1996, Girls Schooling Women Autonomy and Fertility Change in South Asia, London.
10. Ministry of Human Resource Development 1993, Selected Education Statistics 1991-92, New Delhi.
11. The World Bank 1997a, India Achievement and Challenges in Reducing Poverty, Washington DC.

12

Vision of Higher Education in India—A Policy Review

The system and structure of higher education in India suffers from a hangover of colonial rule and still grappling with the problem of modernization. Though the National Knowledge Commission has made well thought out recommendations with a view to improve the scenario with the basic thrust on expansion, enrolment and equity, the system in India does not seem to have addressed certain basic issues as yet that stand as impediments in the path. Expansion by way of increasing the number of institutions of higher learning, though is an ideal proposition, higher education being primarily a state-sponsored activity lack of adequate resources nullify the intent of legislature quite often. Besides, expansion becomes meaningless, if it is only to turn institutions in to factories manufacturing degrees and producing army of unemployed youth. Similarly, enrolment also becomes fruitless activity when students enrol only to obtain certificates and degrees of higher learning for the sake of being called 'educated' as against 'qualified'. The principle of equity in higher learning does not hang in the air. Equity becomes relevant only in the event of institutions producing fruitful results for the youth of the country. As Jawaharlal Nehru said once that 'we cannot have socialism amidst poverty' similarly 'equity' becomes an absurd concept in the middle of system of higher learning that only produces degrees which neither provide jobs nor create opportunities of growth.

The Current Scenario

There are certain basic issues that need to be addressed, if the higher education scenario needs a quantum job in terms of quality and productive character. The percentage of enrolment in higher education in the country is about 18% of the youth between 18 to 23 years of age. It further varies from state to state. It is reported that in 1980 the tertiary enrolment in USA was 55% while, the average for the developing countries was just 5%. In 1995, the rates were 81% for USA and 9% for the rest of the developing countries[1]. It may be stated incidentally that the income gap has also increased during this period. We are in the unenviable position that the enrolment ratio for India is less than the average of the developing countries[2]. However, even in the discouraging percentage of seekers of higher education in the country, more than a half end up with bachelor degrees and jump into job market seeking appointments either in the government sector or in the private. It is a picture of disappointment more often than not.

At the Post Graduate level, the percentage of enrolment is far lesser than 25% than that at under graduate level. This poor enrolment syndrome at Post Graduate level is further marked by percentage of those students who seek degrees and certificates that are of no immediate relevance in so far as opportunities of livelihood are concerned. The degrees are more in the field of humanities like history, sociology, economics, languages, literature, philosophy etc. etc. Why is it that the youth enrol themselves for this sort of unproductive systems of higher learning in terms of livelihood opportunities? It is quite an enigmatic situation one can explain this in the following ways:

(a) The access to higher learning is more easier in the fields of humanities than those of vocational or job-oriented fields. The number of seats in technology and medicine are extremely limited.

(b) It is easier to get through the exams of these courses as they have neither stringent modules of practical learning nor do they have difficult concepts or theorems of complicated comprehension.

(c) Majority of employment opportunities in the government sector including those concerned with All India Services prescribe plain simple graduation as the basic requirement. Besides, almost all the competitive examinations are designed for generalists than specialists. As such it is easier to try ones luck in the government sector than in private where technology, science, management or medicine is a sine-qua-non.

(d) The medium of instruction in these subjects and courses of higher learning is generally vernacular across the country barring a few renowned institutions and colleges that cater to the elite.

(e) Acquisition of degree being seen as acquisition of a status of educated person in the society the easiest way to acquire status is to enrol into these courses which are easily available at every nook and corner of the country. These degrees though un-productive are extremely found acceptable on personal grounds in matters of marriages and social esteem.

(f) The distance education system through open universities and correspondence courses are mostly available in humanities making it easier for drop-outs to acquire a degree without attending to a college or burning the midnight oil.

Lack of Vision

The above being the generally the reasons for proliferation of degrees and institutions connected therewith the system of higher learning with its un-productive nature, is continuing in the country and interestingly the state and society appear to acknowledge this as indices of progress.

But the question remains as to relevance of higher learning when the youth has to struggle for employment with ever increasing inflation and decreasing job opportunities in the private sector ; leaving the question of personality development or a national perspective not to be addressed at this moment. However, it is not to deny the importance of these subjects or courses in terms of their contribution toward building a secular and rational society. The subjects have relevance in their own right in so far as development of a human perspective towards a collective living and community orientation towards the goals of development. The only issue is the lopsided system of higher learning that is resulting in gross waste of man-power which is detrimental to a nation that is struggling hard to address issues of poverty, disease and backwardness for decades.

It is unfortunate that despite decades of independence, the country can not be proud of a uniform education policy which aims at exploring the capabilities of youth with a view to streamline the same as a vital input into the economic development of the country. To begin with, the national policy on education pronounced in the year 1968 deals basically with issues of national integration with cultivation of moral values. A serious thought with regard to economic development of the country with human resources as its engine was conspicuous by its absence in the policy. The policy primarily spelt out a common structure of education throughout the country and introduction of 10+2+3 system besides laying down a common scheme of studies along with science and mathematics as compulsory subjects. The general formulations incorporated in the 1968 policy did not however get translated into a detailed strategy of implementation.[3] As a result, problems of access quality, quantity, utility etc. accumulated over the years and have assumed massive proportions. These are dealt in the new education policy of 1986 and continued to be the focus even in the report of the National Knowledge Commission. Of course, to be fair to the policy makers, the policy contained strong commitment to human values and social justice, besides intention to eradicate rural – urban disparities and promotion of diversification and dispersal of employment opportunities. However, these thoughts could not get translated into action over the years for one reason or the other.

History of Higher Education

Higher education in ancient India was basically influenced by religion and tradition. Historically, flourished at Taxila, Nalanda, Vikramshila (Bihar), Vallabhi (Kathiawad), Kanchi (Tamil Nadu) and Nadia (Bengal). During the British regime, the period 1835 – 1852 is marked by a few colleges in different places in the country including colleges of engineering and medicine. In 1835 Lord Macaulay for the first time advocated closure of institutions of oriental learning as they do not serve the purposes of the modern India. In 1853, the British parliament instituted an enquiry into the status of Indian education. The historical report known as 'Woods Despatch' of July 1854 resulted in establishment of modern universities at Calcutta, Bombay and Madras in 1857. The first Indian education Commission under W.W. Hunters' chairmanship was constituted to deal in aspects of indigenous education, primary, secondary and university education. After the education policy of 1913, almost all provinces were blessed with universities. Banaras Hindu University in 1916 and Mohammedan Anglo Oriental College at Aligarh in 1920 now popularly known as Aligarh Muslim University were the first in the country to be established in tune with the needs of modern education. Later on, universities also started functioning at Mysore, Hyderabad and Patna. The Sergeant Report of 1944 played a catalyst role for further development of national system of education in the country. University Grants Commission formed in 1945 was the brainchild of Sergeant Report.

In the post-independent period, University Education Commission known as Radhakrishnan's Commission was constituted in 1948 which stressed on the need not only for universities. The Commission pointed out that democracy depends for its very life on a high standard of general, vocational and professional education. In 1964, Kothari Commission was constituted to survey and examine the entire field of education which emphasized upon the expansion of higher education, enhance in quality and use of dynamic techniques of management and organization. The 1968 Education Policy was heavily influenced by and based on the recommendations of Kothari Commission. The policies did not have a holistic perspective to address the burning issues of unemployment and poverty. The schemes largely were concerned with expansion of higher education per say with an intention to increase the enrolment of the Indian youth. There was no vision of future of the country in terms of economic and social development though the goals and aspirations did not exclude the same.

The 1986 Policy of Education

The 1986 policy of education is governed more by the spirit of the Indian Constitution especially the Chapter IV – the Directive Principles of State Policy, by way of emphasis on common cultural values and heritage, democracy, secularism, equality of sexes, removal of social barriers, protection of environment etc. etc. Equality of opportunity and removal of prejudices and complexes on the basis of birth is another notable ingredient of the policy. The policy, interestingly envisages international cooperation and peaceful coexistence by motivating younger generations through education true to the ancient sentiment of *Vasudhaiva Kutumbakam*. The policy has an important component of social engineering in as much as its special thrust on education on socially deprived castes and tribes known as scheduled castes and scheduled tribes and other backward sections, areas, minorities and handicapped is concerned. Higher education was given importance in terms of expansion and access.

The policy emphasized redesigning of courses to meet the demands of specialization with a focus on linguistic components and combination of courses. Research in Indology, humanities and social sciences was given adequate support with a view of delve into India's ancient fund of knowledge and with to relate it to contemporary reality implying intense study of Sanskrit and classical languages. Distance learning through open universities was propagated for the first time through the policy, besides making a kind gesture of de-linking degrees from jobs. The policy also aimed at supporting institutions of Gandhian education by way of establishing rural universities - an idea which has never seen in the light of the day. With regard to technical and management education, flexible modular pattern based on credits with provision of multi-point entry was emphasized. Emphasis on vocational education to encourage students towards self-employment by way of training in entrepreneurship is another important feature of the policy of 1986. Innovation, research and development are to be undertaken by all higher technical institutions with an aim to produce quality man-power, with a focus on improving present technologies and developing new indigenous ones to enhance production and productivity.

The views of the policy on the cultural perspective sound to be more conservative in as much as its emphasis on roots of Indian history is concerned. It clearly says,

> *"The pre-occupation with modern technologies cannot be allowed to sever our new generations from the roots of the Indian history and culture. De-culturisation, de-humanisation and alienation must be avoided at all costs. Education can and must give about the fine synthesis between change oriented technologies and the country's culture and tradition."*

The policy is undoubtedly vague in this aspect for it does not define what are the roots of the Indian history and culture. The policy of 1986, one can say, is concerned with the so-called Indianism and social engineering more than its vision for the future of India as nation in the fields of economy and polity and human resource development. No clear cut targets were spelt out in relation to the five-year plan programmes or the market mechanisms and economic growth; and no implementing agencies were nominated to monitor the policy. The Ramamurthy Committee Report of 1990 emphasized on the quality of higher and technical education in real terms not only to make it relevant to the society but also to cater to the needs of competitive industry[4].

The Development of Higher Education

The successive policies of the post independent era have certainly influenced the growth of Higher Education sector in the country. University level institutions have increased from just 18 in 1947 to 307 in 2004. Similarly the enrolment has gone up from 228804 in 1947 to 9463821 in 2003. Faculty-wise enrolment in Arts, was largest with 42.7% while in Commerce and Management, it was 20.7% and in Sciences it was 19.7%.[5] The growth of colleges in absolute number reached a high of 14609 in 2003 where as at the dawn of independence it was just 591[6]. A rapid expansion was witnessed in quantitative terms in the country unparalleled with any country in the world, especially with regard to institutions, teachers. Nevertheless, the percentage of enrolment or coverage between the age group of 17 – 23 was just 7% whereas in Indonesia, it was 11%, Brazil 12%, Mexico 14% and Thailand 19%. The performance of advanced countries is of course phenomenal with U.K at 52%, France at 50%, U.S. 80% and Canada 100%. It is clear that the quantitative achievement of India is basically local and is far below the international average. It is an eye-opener to the policy makers in as much as the aims of universalization of education is concerned not to mention, the qualitative achievement. However, to be fair to the government of independent India it was a Herculean task to educate millions of masses who were never exposed to a universal and formal system of education historically. Still, the policy seems to be suffering from a practical and pragmatic approach to harness the capacities and talents of youth towards achieving economic independence and the overall progress of the nation. Degrees, qualifications and certificates, it appears, were distributed on the basis of enrolment with no regard to the actual usefulness of these testimonials. There is no need to monitor changes in the employment market and to design new approaches to research and development related activities. All the programmes offered by our universities should be directly beneficial to the students in terms of their employability. They should be able to provide what society actually expects from them. Wherever this synchronization is weak, the programmes, courses and the products will not receive social acceptability and credibility[7].

The Plans, Liberalization and Promises by the Government

Thrust areas of IX Plan were as under[8]:

- Measures for quality improvement and modernization of syllabi, renewal of infrastructure.
- Issues of access and relevance would receive attention.
- Conferment of grater autonomy to deserving colleges and professional up gradation of teachers through Academic Staff Colleges.
- Emphasis placed on consolidation and optimal utilization of the existing infrastructure.
- The Open University system, would strive to diversify courses and offerings and gain wider acceptability by upgrading its quality.

The above thrust and focus are general and more or less remained constant through out the X, XIth plans. One fails to find a pragmatic working plan between the areas of focus and the future of the educated youth. The road map seems to be vague as to what needs to be done at what stage. In May, 2004 the UPA Govt. adopted a National Common Minimum Programme (NCMP) as a result of which it has pledged to raise public spending in education to at least 6% of the GDP with at least half this amount being spent on primary and secondary sectors. Naturally the remaining half just 3% is supposed to be spent on Higher Education. Whether this financial commitment was commensurate to the needs of the sector is matter of debate. The liberalization in the country initiated in 90s opened the doors of private players. PPP models received currency across the country in almost all spheres of development including higher education. Private Universities and colleges mostly in Science and technology have mushroomed in the entire country. It appears that at last, the policy makers realized that state ownership on education has not been yielding desired results. The private institutions primarily cater to the needs of the rich and affluent in the country and thereby creating a gross inequal status in the educated besides a great divide between urban and rural. Education has now for all practical purposes, become a business governed by market forces. Whether it is healthy trend, is a million dollar question. The Approach Paper to twelfth plan released by Planning Commission of India admits that the gross enrolment ratio (GER) in higher education must be targeted to increase from nearly 18% to around 25% by the end of 12th Plan i.e 2016-17[9]. The Planning Commission also hopes ambitiously 30% of GER by 2020 while admitting that private universities and colleges have played a major role in increasing enrolment though they are concerns with regard to both equity and quality. All the same, the

Commission is determined to initiate measures to further promote private initiatives while addressing the concerns of quality and equity with a focus on skill development through PPP for employability. The share of enrolment in private higher education is highest in Japan, the Republic of Korea, and Philippines with more than 80%, while in Latin American countries, India, Indonesia and Belgium, it is between 50 – 75%[10]. Though participation of private entrepreneurs in higher education is almost a quarter century old, the UGC and AICTE do not have the break-up of government, government aided private self-financing colleges[11]. Without a database plan process will be at loggerheads to address the issues relevant in PPP models.

Education in India has always been seen, despite loud promises by the policy makers, in isolation. The system of higher learning was never seen as a resource generating programme which can address the burning issues of unemployment, poverty, equality and nation building. No clear cut areas of focus for an all-round economic development were earmarked. The economic inequalities of people were carried straight into the system of higher learning also as the opportunities of learning in productive courses and subjects were confined only to the upper classes. The limited number of seats in courses such as medicine, technology, management, aviation, marine engineering etc. further added to the misery of the poor. Social inequalities in terms of caste, religion and region are not far behind in accentuating and aggravating the misery. The result is a glaring inequality of human beings in the fields of higher learning and consequent degeneration of the system. The concept of equity is reduced to a far cry in the backdrop of the above facts. The policy of education doesn't seem to have a vision aimed at development of the nation and its economy. Most of the states in the country do not have noteworthy and far sighted legislations on education either.

Lessons from China

We have a lot to learn from China - a close neighbour of ours, in as much as the progress in field of education development is concerned. Chinese learning has grown by 20% per year in the last 10 years since 1999, which has reached $ 100 billion with 1.5 million of engineering students graduating from universities in 2006. China has published 1,84,080[12] research papers as on 2008. The country has had a major expansion in education increasing the number of under graduates and holders of doctoral degrees five-fold in last 10 years[13].

This progress of China is not just in isolation. There is a policy and a vision behind the growth of higher education that was governed by the *Four Modernizations* – the goals set forth by Zhou Enlai in 1963 and these were the focus of Chinese government since then, especially under Deng Xiao Ping. These Four Modernizations were in the fields of:

- Agriculture
- Industry
- National Defence
- Science and Technology

The above fields of modernizations were aimed at making China a great economic power by the early 21st century. These reforms essentially emphasized economic self-reliance. The result is more than satisfactory as we look at China in this decade of 21st century. China has emerged today as superpower almost on par with United States in terms of economic development and man-power planning; let alone it's political and military designs.

China has captured almost all markets of the western countries. Major emphasis was laid on vocational and technical skills of the youth in meeting the modernization goals, though humanities were considered equally important. By 1999, primary school education became universal through out China, with a 9-year compulsory education as the top-most priority[14].

With fast expanding horizons of higher education, today China has 47,000 MBAs trained at 62 MBA schools – a course which was unknown in the year 2004. A great number of students apply for international professional qualifications such as ENBA and NPA. Around 10,000 students are enrolled in 47 schools of higher learning including Peking University and Tsinghua University. International cooperation and education exchanges increase every year. China has more students studying abroad than any other country; since 1979, there have been 697,000 Chinese students studying in 103 countries and regions, of whom 1,85,000 have returned after finishing their studies. The number of foreign students studying in China has also increased rapidly; in 2004, over 110,000 students from 178 countries were studying at China's universities. The number of foreigners wanting to study in China has been rising by approximately 20% annually since the reform and opening period began[15]. According to official government figures 195,503 overseas students from 188 countries and regions came to study on the mainland in 2007 although the number is believed to be somewhere around the 300,000, because the government's figures do not include students studying at private language schools.

This makes China the world's sixth largest study abroad destination. Currently China has around 1000 universities. Some universities, such as Beijing University and Tsinghua University, have already gained international reputation for outstanding teaching and research facilities. China has signed agreements with almost 40 countries such as France, Great Britain, the United States of America, Russia, etc., to recognize each others diplomas.

China has laws regulating the system of education including the Regulation on Academic Degrees, the Compulsory Education Law, the Teachers Law, the

Education Law, the Law on Vocational Education, and the Law on Higher Education. India has a long way to go in this respect.

Undoubtedly, it is a quantum jump that China has achieved in the field of higher education in the last few decades purely on the basis of a vision and a long-term policy to harness the talent and capacities of the youth of the nation. The absence of Four Modernizations replication in India is certainly a severe drawback that is visibly felt in the field of higher education in India. Education in India is a concurrent subject in the constitution which empowers both centre and state governments to make legislations. Probably this is the most important cause for not evolving a common Education Law or policy with a view to develop the human resources and harness young talent in the country.

Where do we Stand?

Let us briefly examine as to what are the basic pitfalls or drawbacks in the education scenario of India. Formal education through a structured pattern of pedagogic content and certification was unknown to the country until the British arrived. The reforms introduced by the British in the late 19th century have certainly created a foundation for formal system of education through 10+2 model. The same is carried forward until the 20th century by all the state governments. Major emphasis and attention was given only to primary and secondary education while the higher education was confined to urban areas - primarily catering to the needs of elite. The post independent era has witnessed, however, a consorted thinking across the state to expand higher education so as to reach to every corner of the country in the best possible way.

Education Remained Aimless

Education policies in the 20th century have been mainly focussing on enrolment with out a concern for 'Lab to Land' practical results. National economic priorities were not connected to Education sector unlike in China. Increase in the number of colleges and institutions of higher learning has been phenomenally seen across the country. Nevertheless, it was mostly the Humanities which were taught and in which young people graduated. Even legal education was not within the reach of common people until the last two decades. There has never been a vision to encourage growth of education with an aim to develop human resources that can contribute to the economic development of the country. Productive learning was largely confined to the affluent sections of the society.

The adequate emphasis on higher education in terms of employability has always been absent in almost all the five-year plans of the country. The budgetary allocations have been minimal to the field of higher education, both in the central and state budget while on the contrary; school education has been given considerable importance. The question of enrolment in the institutions in the field of higher learning has always been addressed in isolation with out regard for the future of pass outs.

Inadequate Job Market

Higher education is a sine-qua-non for securing employment in a competitive environment both in the government and private sectors. The former has so much of flexibility to accommodate almost all graduates, at least in trying their luck, irrespective of their subjects whereas the latter primarily requires scientific and technical knowledge and expertise. The poor growth of private sector until the liberalisation programme of the state in 1990s is another important reason for the poor growth of the higher education sector in technical and professional courses. It is also a fact that even with fast growing private sector, the infrastructure for higher learning in terms of institutions, hostels, laboratories or research centres, has not received required attention with the result that there is a cut-throat competition to secure seats in these institutions. But for the seat reservations to Dalits and backward classes, these institutions would have only been catering to the upper caste and elites of Indian society. Still large number of aspirants for these courses end up pursuing Humanities as they could not succeed in securing admissions in the above subjects. The result is a large army of unemployed youth with unproductive degrees trying their fortune in the government sector employment that has its own limits. Out sourcing of production process by industries, a trend catching up in 21st century across the world has its impact in India too. Industries no longer need permanent work force including white collared employment. Labour is more a commodity now than a factor of production. The educated need jobs to fend for themselves and plan their future. Or else what meaning a degree or a certificate has?

Medium of Instruction

Language has played its own role in reducing the employment opportunities of the youth in the country, we must admit. In a nation with around 20 official languages in different states and with Hindi as the official language at the centre besides English, it is anybody's imagination as to how an aspirant with a degree obtained through a vernacular medium can be successful in trying his luck outside his own state. After all states in India have been formed purely on linguistic basis. Though English remains as a common lingua franca access to English knowledge is measured in terms of one's economic capacities as english medium education is a costly affair for a common man. Higher learning in majority of states in the country is still in the vernacular medium. It makes it difficult for a student to reach out to the rest of the world and learn for most of the quality learning material is available in English. Unfortunately in some states, especially in the heartland of Hindi speaking population, English is considered as a remnant of slavery that Indians were subjected to by the

British. In these states, academics get politicized unfortunately when ever the question of medium of instruction arises. But it also happens to be surprisingly a fact that the politicians and leaders who advocate vernacular medium, prefer to send their own children to English medium schools and colleges. It is high time that a serious thought is given to the question of medium if we really want a perceivable change in the field of higher learning. Why should English language be the property of the rich and the elite alone? A language which has contributed to the growth of nationalism and has been responsible greatly for the growth of freedom movement across the country need not be discouraged or shunned as a colonial legacy. In some states such as West Bengal, Odisha and southern states, English is still accepted as a medium of education in Universities and the results have been glaringly positive and encouraging. Today, even China has made it mandatory to learn English in the primary and secondary school education and it is especially with a view to create man-power that can outsmart that of the rest of the world.

Educators to be Educated?

Teaching profession in the institutions of higher learning is characterised more by factors of compulsion than by choice. The educated youth of the country aspire more for positions in the government service as it has an advantage and sense of empowerment. Private sector with limited job opportunities mainly accommodates graduates in science and technology or management. The unfortunate aspirants in both sectors prefer to take up teaching jobs as that is an immediate source of livelihood, no matter whether they have an aptitude for the same or not. Teaching profession demands qualifications though such as NET, doctoral, research degrees etc., while at the same time it cannot strictly lay down a test for aptitude to teach. When teaching professions are chosen out of helplessness by the educated youth, the quality of teaching or the involvement in pedagogic exercise cannot be guaranteed in institutions of higher learning. However, this is not to discredit the teaching community as there is equally a sizeable section with academic prowess and magnificent contribution in the field. All that is to say is that techniques of teaching and the quality of the content can be better monitored by strict implementation of training programmes for the teaching community connected with higher learning.

Examination Reforms

The system of examinations is an area often debated across the country for years. Examination reforms is one aspect that calls for immediate attention of the policy makers in the country. Though memory is an unavoidable component of learning, development of analytical capabilities with a good IQ is very essential. It is unfortunate to distribute degrees on the basis of written examinations which students participate in mostly by learning by heart the material available in the market. It is a pity that private institutions of higher learning constantly strive to bring out the best results by qualifying 100% of their students, no matter, whether the content of learning is useful or whether there is any positive change in the personality of the student. The market is flourishing with private institutions mushrooming all over the country, so much so that they sponsor expensive commercial Ads in the print and electronic media. Higher learning no longer seems to be a noble field of intellectual excellence or personality development, useful for the country and the nation. It has become more a field of business with supply and demand as the chief factors.

Expansion and Access: Victims of Politics

Expansion of higher education in the country has its own tales of woe. The regional imbalances which we witness in the field of economic development have their presence in the field of higher learning too. Expansion as a principle though accepted by all, the political society of the country tends to impose restrictions for sectarian gains with a personal agenda. Many states in the country do not have required infrastructure to meet the needs of expansion in comparison to their better counterparts in the country. The system of coalition governments often accommodates interests of particular section or region and try to placate the forces that matter for the stability of the government. Incidentally, higher learning institutions in the field of medicine, technology, science, management etc. need clearances and permissions from the central bodies. Political factors influenced by non secular forces have a predominant role to play in ensuring the fulfilment of sectarian interests. This is a very unhealthy trend that one has to live with in the largest democracy of the world. Besides expansion, the principle of equity also suffers as a victim of political compulsions. Social engineering is the trend of the day. However, a lot remains to be achieved still in terms of equitable distribution of gains in the field of higher learning so that all the hitherto disadvantaged groups and sections of people receive the fruits equally. This is an area of larger debate.

Last Word

The above being some major impediments on the road to development of higher education in India, the same need to be removed in due course of time with a concerted effort by the policy makers of the country. The field of education has number of issues to be addressed which cannot be accomplished overnight. All that is required is a strong political will as we have seen in case of China that can make a drastic difference in the ongoing system. Higher learning is not for learning per se. It is an important input and a factor for the overall progress of the nation, be it in the fields of economy, polity or society. Human resources are extremely important for the development of democratic modern nation as opposed to a metropolis of the colonial era. The latter progressed economically by a constant mechanism and system of plundering its colonies, be it the British or the French. These nations did not have to struggle to achievement of their economic goals as they siphoned off the resources of their colonies successfully into their own nations. On the contrary, countries like China have a glorious history of struggle through reforms backed by nationalistic vision to achieve economic development. India is one nation which can surely borrow the example from China at least in the area of higher education. It is high time the country has formulated a vision and a policy for development of human resources especially higher education with an aim to achieve economic development and reduce the percentage of unemployment. The policy must have pragmatism as its driving force in place of party manifesto or populist stunt. It is also necessary for all the political parties and regional factions to understand that their interests would survive only when the country survives as a nation and its youth as the agents of change. There is no dearth of intellectuals, professionals and statesmen in India, who can come with best alternatives and fruitful proposals only if the policy makers have patience and concern. Let us not forget that one citizen could make a great difference to the development of this country in the last 20 years in the field of electronics, communications and information technology. Mr. Sam Pitroda's contribution to India will never be forgotten till the eternity. The Knowledge Commission's recommendations, to begin with, can seriously be implemented across the country in all sincerity.

REFERENCES

1. The World Bank Report 2002, pp. 46-47.
2. V.C. Kulandaiswamy, Ibid, pp. 20-21.
3. www.education.nic.in/cd50years/g/t/49)

4. Professor Dayanand Dongaonkar. "Issues in Higher Education", in K.Venkat Subrahmanyan, Ed.– *Issues in Higher Education,* ICFAI University Press, Hyderabad, 2004, pp. 12.
5. UGC Annual Report 2000-2001.
6. University Handbook 2003.
7. K.Venkat Subrahmanyan, Ibid, pp. 14.
8. Website : www.education.nic.in
9. Issues for the Approach in 12th Plan, Planning Commission of India, New Delhi, pp. 5.
10. "Higher Education : The Lessons of Experience", The World Bank Report; (1994) pp. 36.
11. V.C. Kulandaiswamy. *Recognition of Higher Education in India;* ICFAI University Press, Hyderabad, 2006.
12. Su, Xiaohuan (2002), China to overtake US on science' in two years, BBC World news, ISBN 7801139933.
13. China's Book in Higher Education graphic in The New York Times based on information from China's Ministry of Education, April 28, 2005.
14. Su, Xiaohuan (2002), Education in China : reforms and innovations, ISBN 7801139933.
15. Number of Foreign Students in China rises 20% annually. China.org.cn.2006-01-19. http://china.org.cn/english/international/155726.htm. Retrieved 2009-07-14.

13

Laws, Enforcement and Disasters in Urban Areas

The increase in number of Public Interest Litigations in the country with regard to issues such as general safety of the people, life and liberty is an important indication of the collective concern with regard to human life and basic human rights. Article 21 of Indian constitution makes it explicitly clear that the life and liberty of a citizen cannot be taken away except by a procedure established by law. In other words, it is a fundamental right enshrined in Chapter III which casts a burden on the state and every individual to ensure that the life and liberty of a fellow citizen cannot be taken away. Article 32 is again a fundamental right which lays down the jurisdiction of the Supreme Court to direct the state to comply with article 21 besides other fundamental rights.

Disasters are of two kinds i.e., natural and man-made. Natural disasters are an act of vis major (divine act), whereas man-made disasters are absolutely an act of either negligence, sabotage or conspiracy. The former cannot be averted by human capacity whereas the latter can be. Natural disasters are often unexpected and their impact causes extensive damage across the territory. For instance, earthquakes, floods, landslides, Tsunamis etc. give little or practically no time to react to ensure safety of human beings. The 2004 Tsunami of the southern coast of India, claiming several thousands of lives was a catastrophe unexpected by any quarters of society or government. Similarly, the earthquake of Gujarat or that of Lathur in Maharashtra are equally damaging calamities which the people are still struggling to overcome. The man-made disasters result due to irresponsibility and recklessness on the part of the management responsible for ensuring safety of the locality. The major man-made disaster in India dates back to 1984, when the Union Carbide, an American company in Bhopal, engaged in manufacture of fertilizers, emitted huge amounts of methyl isocyanides in the middle of the night in the city claiming more than 10,000 lives. It has permanently in-capacitated and disabled thousands more.

URBAN DISASTERS

Urban areas generally known as municipalities, metropolis or cities are more susceptible for man-made disasters as lakhs of people inhabit in these areas. Bhopal gas tragedy is one such example for a man-made disaster in urban areas. The contaminated and poisonous gases leaked by Shriram Fertilizers in New Delhi was another case of possible urban disasters, which the Supreme Court adjudicated upon in *Ashok Mehta vs Union of India*. Urban disasters cause more damage to lives and property than the natural calamities that occur in rural areas. Because the habitation in rural areas is scanty and gives more escape routes under the open sky be it floods, earthquakes or Tsunamis. On the contrary, the population in the urban locality such as cities and towns is normally trapped within the four corners of the locality with little escape in emergency. Crowded localities, narrow roads, high rising buildings, petrol pumps, gas stations, railway lines etc. are most probable messengers of death in the event of panic as people run for life. Urban areas need more concentrated planning and action, firstly to avoid the disasters that are primarily man-made and secondly to minimise the damage especially to life, if one takes place.

Towns and cities are in a way are the showpieces of development, civilization, growth and excellence and as so naturally they expand by leaps and bounds due to massive influx of migrants from rural areas in search of better life, employment, health and security. Is the law and the State or law enforcing machinery effective in ensuring safety to the life and liberty of the citizens is a million dollar question that needs to be addressed. What laws are made and how they are implemented and what safeguards are provided against violation of safety norms for industries have always been issues of public interest in all urban areas. Let us examine in detail as to what is the impact of the laws and role of the enforcement agencies in addressing the issues by focussing on relevant areas where improvement can be made by renewed thoughts and efforts.

LEGAL AND TECHNO-LEGAL FRAMEWORK

For the first ever time in India an Act called the Disaster Management Act was brought in to force with effect from 25th December 2005. The Act aims at providing for effective management of Disasters and matters connected there with. The institutional frame work and mechanisms required for drawing up and implement plans to control and mitigate Disasters ware provided in the act. According to the Act a National Disaster management Authority (NDMA) under the leadership of Prime Minister and a State Disaster Management Authority (SMDA) under the chairmanship of Chief Minister. Similarly at District level the District Magistrate will head the District Disaster Management Authority (DDMA). Constitution of National Executive Committee (NEC) headed by the Home Secretary, is an important aspect of the act. Besides, the act had made provision for National Institute of Disaster Management and National Disaster Response Force. All the Ministries and Departments that are connected with the subject of disaster in one way or the other are all responsible to draw up Department-wise plans in accordance with National Disaster Management Plan.

THE DISASTER MANAGEMENT POLICY

The National Institute for Disaster Management in India came up with the policy on Disaster Management in the country. The status report by the organization extensively discusses the nature of disasters and the detailed arrangements to meet the challenges by the government. Disaster management is a multi-disciplinary activity involving a number of departments and agencies spanning across all sectors of development. The policy has been drafted with a changed focus integrating disaster mitigation with developmental planning in order to minimise loss of lives and property specifically for the poor and vulnerable sections. The policy emphasizes on a unified action both by central and state governments. The salient features of the policy are as under :

(a) A pro-active approach towards preparedness to prevent and mitigate the disaster and its impact.

(b) Both central and state governments will set-apart resources under the plan addressing vulnerability, reduction and preparedness.

(c) The on-going developmental schemes and programmes will have disaster management designs incorporated within.

(d) Community involvement by awareness generation, capacity-building and empowerment.

(e) Close interaction with corporate sector, NGOs and the media Institutional structures for appropriate training to Disaster Managers at various levels.

(f) Standard operating procedures for managing specific disasters.

(g) Construction designs to be as per the Indian standards enforced.

(h) All public places, such as hospitals, railway stations, airports, bus-stands need to be reviewed in terms of risk management and preparedness.

(i) Disaster management course to be revised with stress on mitigation and preparedness.

(j) Promoting international cooperation in the areas of disaster management.

All the state governments in India have been advised by the centre to come up with their own acts, making provisions for adequate powers for the authorities in mitigation, preparedness and response. Gujarat and Bihar are probably the first to enact disaster management acts whereas the other states are still at the stage of drafting. The disaster management code is a new name given to the relief rules or codes existing in different states. Accordingly the state governments have been advised to rename as Disaster Management Codes. These codes are necessary for drawing up detailed mitigation plans along with preparedness in addition to response and relief. It is heartening to know that the existing Director of National Institute of Disaster Management has headed a committee which has drafted a Model Disaster Management Code and is circulated to the States.

The technical aspect of the disaster management has been taken seriously by almost all the state governments in the country and consequently successive batches of officers, both at decision making level and at the field were trained periodically in various training institutes and colleges across the country in short terms courses on disaster management. Besides a disaster management institute has been established in almost every State's headquarters in the capital.

Let us examine various issues that cause concern with regard to disasters in urban areas and explore legal and administrative possibilities in order to firstly prevent the disaster and secondly, to mitigate or avoid possible loss to human life and precious property and infrastructure of the society.

CAUSES OF DISASTERS IN URBAN AREAS

Urban areas in the country are characterized firstly by the increased number of people inhabiting, secondly by pecca constructed houses and thirdly by vast infrastructure such as electricity supply, railway lines, sewerage systems, public places with increased congregation of crowds. A disaster occurs in urban areas when these characteristics of a city are thoroughly disturbed or endangered overnight causing immense damage to life, liberty and property, i.e. normally beyond repair. Some of the causes for such calamities can be listed as under :-

(a) Industrial disasters such as poisonous gas leak, massive fire, hazardous waste disposal causing radiation and pollution of water bodies.

(b) Transport disasters such as collision of public transport systems such as derailment of trains, air crash etc.

(c) Unforeseen earthquake causing havoc in the city such as the one we have seen in Jabalpur in 1997 and in Gujarat in 2001.

The above are some of the disasters normally expected or unexpected to occur in urban areas. Barring natural calamities such as earthquakes or cyclones, majority of disasters in urban areas are known as man-made which could be avoided provided the legal framework to handle the subject on 'disaster' is well designed and the enforcement of laws is ensured without fail. Let us examine as to what could be the areas that require renewed thrust and emphasis.

(i) The Laws for Safety – How Effective are they?

The National Disaster Management Act as we have discussed earlier provides for institutional mechanisms for implementation of Disaster Management plans with a collective participation of all the departments and with coordinated efforts. Though the Act is perfect in its own right, what is more important is to make arrangements that are necessary to avoid and to prevent through a legal framework. For instance establishment of industries near by thickly populated cities or towns is an open invitation to large scale disasters especially in case of industries such as Sponge iron plants, Blast Furnace units of steel industries, chemicals and fertilizers based manufacturing units or those which consume substantial amount of electricity, coal and water. It is a tragedy that a large number of towns and cities in the country, some or the other industry is situated in the middle of the city or close to the city either engaged in hazardous manufacturing or potentially dangerous materials. Most of the urban areas being old cities, the Town and Country Planning Acts and its regulations are reduced to nullity in addressing the location issue of these industries.

The municipalities in the country are local self governments ascribed with the status of the State as per Article 12 of the Constitution. The municipalities have Municipal Laws to accord or reject permissions for establishment of industries or hazardous concerns within the city or within the limits of the city in order to ensure clean air, safe drinking water and effective sewerage disposal systems. However, ever increasing sanitation problems, contaminated drinking water, good number of tanneries working on the banks of big rivers close to cities, unsafe and unhygienic disposal of bio-waste into drinking water sources such as rivers, streams etc. raise questions with regard to either the efficacy of the laws or the performance of the municipal bodies in the country. These establishments are potential causes for disasters at any point of time. Often the local authorities succumb to political pressures and grant permissions for industries or concerns that could be disastrous. The District enforcement machinery and the concerned departments which have the authority to certify the safety aspect of industries (Department of Labour, Chief Inspector of Factories, Department of

Industries, the State Electricity Board etc.) often turn a blind eye to the faulty safety systems either motivated by vested interests or guided by political pressures. For instance the Chief Inspector of Factories as per section 9 of Factories Act, has immense powers to reject a design of a manufacturing unit or factory if it does not adhere to the norms of safety, health and security of the workforce as laid down from sections 11 to 48. But rarely do we come across some cases where permissions are refused for unsafe industries are action initiated. Similarly, the State Electricity Board of any State does not seem to refuse supply of power to new and upcoming industries or even existing industries which violate the safety norms.

It is worth mentioning here that the controversial pain-killer drug Diclophenic compound banned across the world by World Health Organization is still in use in India permitted officially by the concerned authorities. The veterinary use of this drug on live stock had an indirect result of massive disappearance of vultures in India in the last 20 years which is scientifically co-related by the fact that the carcasses eaten by vultures contain deadly diclophenic which cause slow death to the vultures. Let us not forget that vultures were the natural scavengers in the world saving the mankind from disastrous epidemics. The ecological balance is after all an integral part of disaster management.

(ii) The Laws against Unsafe Constructions

Crowded inhabitations in cities fall victim to sudden disasters as the buildings, civil constructions, narrow roads do not permit quick evacuation of the population. The Town and Country Planning Act of States lays down strict guidelines with regard to permissions for house constructions or any other buildings in the municipal areas. Barring few metro and mega cities, majority of medium and small towns and cities have un-controlled illegal constructions making mockery of norms of constructions prescribed by the relevant acts. These urban areas are characterised by congested public places, narrow lanes and roads and busy market places. These are potential threat to safety and security to people at large. In the event of any unforeseen calamity which can cause large scale damage to human life, these cities and towns will suffer the worst part of it. Despite the existence of well drafted acts and rules in this regard, still the scenario goes uncontrolled primarily due to lenient law enforcing machineries and authorities. To make matters worse, communal sentiments are often whipped up on strong grounds of faith and sentiment such as temples, mosques, churches and other places of religious worship making it difficult for the state machinery to remove encroachments or control dangerous unlawful constructions. Recently in Sabarimalai at Kerala a human disaster occurred claiming many lives during a stampede at the temple of Swamy Ayyappa. Similar incidents keep occurring in one corner or the other in the country from time to time. These are disasters purely man-made and are consequences of negligence of state machinery and violation of norms by the civil society.

The aims and objectives of Town and Country Planning Act is to ensure healthy and safe living by making a master plan of the land by prescribing land use pattern across the city. It provides for human habitations, parks, amusement places, schools, institutions etc. besides also making provision for industrial parks or estates separately away from human habitations. An average construction in a plot is supposed to be broadly 2/3rd of plot leaving 1/3rd around the plinth area for air circulation and unobstructed vision for the neighbours. Roads and lanes are also prescribed with specific width so that vehicular traffic can be smooth without causing danger to human life and property. Owners of the building are supposed to obtain valid clearances from the authorities before starting the construction. Unfortunately the rules are more often flouted than complied with. Here the role of the civil society and that of law enforcing machinery comes under question calling for a better and lawful responsibility at both ends.

(iii) Laws Against Pollution of Air and Water:

The Central Govt. has enacted way back in 70s and 80s three important acts to ensure pollution free air and water for citizens. These are;

1. Water (Prevention and Control of Pollution) Act 1974.
2. Air (Prevention and Control of Pollution) Act 1981.
3. The Environment (Protection) Act 1986.

These Acts are enforced across the country and the provisions of the Acts are binding on all State Govts. These Acts are basically aimed at preventing any water borne or air borne disasters by prescribing rules and regulations to check pollution levels of water and air. The Acts provide for State Air laboratory and State Water laboratory for testing samples of water and air collected from industrial establishments and other concerns. Analysts appointed for this purpose make recommendation for action against pollution.

Sections 3, 4 and 5 of Air (Prevention and Control of Pollution) Act 1981 provide for constitution of Boards both at Centre and State for Prevention and Control of Pollution of air. Apart from official members the boards consist of specialists in fields of Agriculture, Industry, Trade, Fisheries, and labour. The main functions of the Boards are to improve the quality of air and prevent, control or abate air pollution. The Boards advise both Central and State governments respectively on matters of improving the quality of air and prevention of pollution by initiating a nation-wide programme. The Boards collect and disseminate information related to air pollution and organize training for persons engaged in programmes related to control of air pollution. Under section 18, the central government has powers to issue directions to central or state boards or to State Governments, with regard to air pollution and control.

These directions are mandatory and include any other direction in addition to the functions assigned to the Boards[1]. Section 21 of Air (Prevention and Control of Pollution) Act 1981 mandates that no person without the previous consent of Board operate any industrial plant specified in the schedule in the air pollution control area. Section 22 of the act provides that no person shall discharge or cause or permit to be discharged the emission of any air pollution in excess of the standards by state boards of clause 9 of sub-section 1 of section 17. The Board can move to the court of Metropolitan Magistrate or the Sessions Magistrate for action against the person violating the law. The Act provides for strict punishments and penalties from section 31 to 43 including imprisonment which extend to 3 months.

The Water (Prevention and Control of Pollution) Act 1974 has almost similar provisions that are made in Air (Prevention and Control of Pollution) Act 1981. As a matter of fact, the Water Act is a predecessor to the Air Act.

The Environment (Protection) Act 1986 is another milestone in the campaign against pollution and endangerment to natural sources of human life such as water, air, earth and eco-system. The Stockholm Environment Conference in 1972 is the watershed for a campaign to protect environment at the international level. Environmental protection has a strong bearing on prevention and control of disasters. The parliament has passed a number of anti pollution acts including Forest Conservation Act 1980, Wild life Protection Act 1972, Water Act 1974 and Air Acts 1981, Silent Valley Protection Act 1979, besides creating a separate Ministry of Environment to protect the nature and environment. Section 2(a) of Environment Act includes water, air and land and the inter-relationship which exists among and between all these elements and human beings along with flora and fauna. The Supreme Court in M.C. Mehta vs Union of India[2] as observed that acidic emissions into the atmosphere also amount to environment pollution. Similarly in Subha Rao vs State of Himachal Pradesh[3], the Supreme Court has observed that the bone factory polluting the environment by its pungent smell amounts to environmental pollution. In Vellore, Citizens vs Union of India, the Supreme Court held that the main purpose of this act is to create authority or authorities with adequate powers to control pollution and protect environment[4].

Despite well laid provisions for preventing and controlling air and water pollution, violation of these basic human rights is common in the country especially in urban areas. One wonders as to what these Boards are doing to prevent pollution? The answer is not surprising. The heads of these Boards are appointed more on political grounds than on qualifications they possess. The State and the Central governments, though, avowedly exhibit commitments to the health and safety of citizens, the appointments to these Boards are often guided by political considerations and sectarian interests. The result is dismal performance causing potential threat to public life and safety. It is unfortunate that in the country though we have strict laws and stringent punishments, it is practically difficult to blow the whistle or bring the culprits to the book. The law enforcing machineries and the political leadership are primarily answerable to such a dilemma of Indian administration.

(iv) The Judicial Activism

The Indian Judiciary has time and again played a very important role in issuing directions for protections of environment and for provision of pollution-free air and water. In a case[5] their lordships have enabled citizens to bring action against public bodies to force them to be vigilant to keep the environment free from pollution. It is a landmark decision which has awakened the public towards their right to live in a pollution-free environment.

In another case[6] the Court has made a detailed order regarding the working of the limestone quarries in the Dehradun-Mussorie belt.

In M.C. Mehta vs Union of India[7], the Supreme Court passed a very important order for the protection and preservation of the environment. In this case, there was a major leakage of the ileum gas from one of the units of Shriram Food and Fertilizers and as result of which several person were affected. The Court held that reasonable approach is essential for economic development and well being of the people.

In the Ganga Water Pollution case[8] the petitioner M.C. Mehta, sought to enforce the Fundamental Rights to a clean and hygienic environment as a part of Article 21 of the Constitution. In this case, the Supreme Court directed the Tanneries to install primary treatment plant, failing which the tanneries would have to stop the business.

Further in M.V. Sharma Vs. Bharat Electricity[9] the Supreme Court laid down guidelines for the protection of worker's health. It also held that living in polluted environment endangers the very life of human beings, animals and plants.

In Damodar Rao Vs. Municipal Corporation[10], the Court observed that the enjoyment of life and its attainment and fulfilment guaranteed by Article 21 of the Constitution, embraces the protection and preservation of nature's gifts without which the life cannot be enjoyed. There can be no reason why practice of violent extinguishment of life alone should be regarded as violative atmosphere caused by environment pollution and spoliation should also be regarded as amounted to violation of Article 21 of the Constitution.

The increasing role of judiciary in controlling the state actions for the purpose of protecting air, water and environment amply speak for the fact that the state and its law enforcing mechanisms are failing on and off in protecting the citizens from potential causes of disasters. The judicial legislation is becoming often the only recourse for a common man against the corrupt and insincere law enforcing authorities in the country. This is a serious matter of concern for a democratic government.

(v) Maintenance of Law and Order

With un-systematic sprawling of human settlements and business establishments in the cities, one more aspect which causes extreme concern is the issue of law and order. Disasters hit the worst way those cities and towns which have the least respect for maintenance of law and order. Unregulated crowd gatherings, massive rallies without permissions, unbridled encroachments and let loose criminal elements can cause severe damage to life and property when a calamity such as earthquake, sudden cyclonic storm or bursting of a Dam with substantial amount of water takes place. Constant patrolling especially in the nights can check the criminal elements from possible sabotage activities that could result in disasters. Effective surveillance of city life by police department day in and day out will help warning the innocent crowds to save themselves from disasters. For instance, the Bhopal gas tragedy has also an element of poor surveillance by the police who could have warned the crowds hours before the leak of deadly gas. In a short notice people unfortunately fell victim while asleep especially the homeless and the poor on the footpaths and pavements whereas, while others succumbed to the calamity while sleeping in their homes.

Crowded places such as markets, parks, theatres, railway stations etc. need fore-warning systems and alerting apparatus to educate people well in advance and inform timely about the possible disaster that can occur. Safe escape routes or shelters are a must in public places in order to protect the people from the disaster. It is a pity that today almost all cities despite getting over-crowded have hardly any disaster management infrastructure, shelters, warning systems or escape routes. The ever increasing traffic jams can vouch for this fact that in the event of a disaster, the population on the road can hardly have an escape to life. It is the duty of the law enforcing machinery including the civic administration and police to ensure the safety of the citizens especially in mega cities.

Terrorist attacks are another worst man-made disasters. The Mumbai serial blasts in 1993 and the recent ones in Delhi, Ahmedabad and Hyderabad are the worst examples of the terrorist attacks on innocent citizens. Natural disasters are a divine act with no mens rea against mankind while the terrorist attacks are guided by hatred nurtured by unsocial and criminal elements in the name of faith or ideology. It is a serious issue of law and order that the state has to address with sufficient care and caution. Left wing extremist activities like naxalite attacks killing hundreds continuously in various parts of the country are another example of man-made disaster. It is high time that the nation rose to the occasion and seriously tackle these issues of terrorism and human holocaust.

Provisions of IPC and Cr. P.C for Public Safety and Security

The two major acts that concerned with the penal law and procedure namely Indian Penal Code and Criminal Procedure Code have sufficient provisions to pre-empt and prevent any likely act of any citizen or or an organization which can be potentially a cause for disaster. These provisions are as under :

(a) Section 188 of IPC makes dis-obedience to an order promulgated by the public servant as an offence if such dis-obedience causes or tends to cause danger to human life, health or safety. The punishment provided is imprisonment for a term which may extent to 6 months. The man-made disasters often caused by negligence and irresponsibility of industrial concerns can be checked by public authorities under these provision.

(b) Public nuisance as defined in section 268 of IPC includes commission and omission which can cause injury, danger to public or community in general. Section 269 provides a punishment of imprisonment up to 6 months for the negligent Act likely to spread infection of disease dangerous to life.

(c) Section 272 of IPC provides for punishment up to 6 months imprisonment for any person who adulterates any articles of food or drink which becomes harmful for human life.

(d) Section 277 of IPC deals with the offence of polluting water or public spring or reservoir and prescribes of punishment up to 6 months imprisonment.

(e) Section 285 of the IPC prohibits pulling down or repairing any building which can cause probable danger to human life and makes it punishable with an imprisonment of 6 months.

(f) The Cr. PC, from sections 133 to 143 defines 'public nuisance' as obstruction, risk and injury of life of public at large and provides for action against the offenders. These include obstruction, nuisance to public way, river, any trade or keeping goods injurious to public health, and any tank, well or excavation adjacent to any public place. Section 133 authorizes a District Magistrate, or Sub-divisional Magistrate or Executive magistrate to pass an order as he may think fit to remove such public nuisance. In case of Krishna Gopal Vs. State of M.P 1986[11], the Indore bench of High Court held that the Caplic Factory and its Boiler were releasing huge quantity of smoke, ash and obnoxious gases which cause public nuisance.

These are some of the provisions that can be taken help of by the public authorities as a precautionary and pre-emptive move to avoid any possibility of disaster in thickly populated cities and towns. But it is unfortunate that the Executive Magistrates do not take advantage of these provisions well in advance either by ignorance or by lack of sincerity. Even if they do, it is when it is either too late or by vested interests of pleasing or dis-pleasing some sections or the other.

Conclusion

As we have discussed in the fore-going pages, disasters in highly inhabited cities and townships occur mostly by human error of negligence which are known as man-made calamities. However there are Laws made to enable the State to prevent or control the Disasters. Environmental protection with special focus on water, air and infrastructure is an integral part of and complementary to disaster managemeny. It is heartening that the Disaster Management Act is enforced and almost all state governments have risen to the occasion to deal with aspects of prevention and mitigating disasters with a special focus. However, what is more important is a holistic approach to urban disasters. This includes an overall strategy to preserve air, water and environment free from pollution and danger. The existing laws with regard to safety of public life in terms of Town and Country Planning, Transportation, Law and order and control of pollution of natural sources of life need to be implemented and enforced in letter and spirit without fear or favour. Though it is often orchestrated that the civil society with people's participation has a decisive role to protect the life and liberty of citizens from possible disasters, I personally feel that it is the State and its enforcing machinery which has the prime role to play. Nevertheless, education and communication with regard to preparedness in the event of disasters is of course very essential and must be imparted and given to all citizens. Besides, it can form a part of regular curriculum of school education.

As it is said that 'prevention is better than cure', all of us have a responsibility to act in accordance with the demand of the situation and state of affairs we are living in and do the best in our own right and in our capacity to help the campaign for Disaster Management.

REFERENCES

1. K. Kuppuswamy vs State, AIR, 1998 KAMP 281.
2. A.I.R 1997 S.C 734.
3. A.I.R 1989 S.C. 171.
4. A.I.R 1996 S.C. 2715.
5. Source : Ratlam Municipality Vs. Vardhi Chand, A.I.R. 1980, S.C. 1622.
6. Rural Litigation Vs. State of U.P.F.I.R. 1985, S.C. 652.
7. A.I.R 1957, S.C. 465.
8. M.C. Mehta vs Union of India, A.I.R. 1988 S.C. 1037.
9. A.I.R 1987, S.C. 1792.
10. A.I.R 1987, A.P. 171.
11. Criminal Law Journal 376.

14
The Politics of Global Warming

Global warming is an unfortunate phenomena that has surfaced in the second half of the 20th century and threatening the very existence of the Mother Earth. The Green House effect otherwise known as the excessive quantity of CO_2 in the atmosphere resulting in preservation of excessive heat on the planet has caused warming of the Mother Planet. In simple terms, for a layman, it is more heat generated causing variations in weather cycle and endangering the lives of the human beings by way of melting of glaciers and the polar ice depositions thereby rising the level of the oceans. Now it is no longer a secret that Himalayan glaciers have melted more than 30% from 1960s till now and even the United States of America the Polar Bear is declared an endangered species as the glaciers in the north pole have melted considerably due to global warming. The logical consequences of global warming are excessive heat, change of weather cycle, depletion of Ozone layer, exposure to harmful ultra-violet rays of the sun, acid rains destroying the forests etc. etc.

Climate change is one the greatest environmental, social and economic threats facing the planet. Climate change is a "change of climate which is attributed directly or indirectly to human activity that alters the composition of the global atmosphere and which is in addition to natural climate variability observed over comparable time periods".[1] The warming of the climate as evident from the observations of increase in global average air and sea temperatures, widespread melting of snow and ice and rising global mean sea level. The earth's average surface temperature has risen by 0.76°C since 1850. Most of the warming that has occurred over the last 50 years is very likely to have been caused by industrial activities. Projected global warming in this century is likely to trigger serious consequences for humanity and other life forms. Human activities that contribute to climate charge and *Global Warming* include in particular, the burning of fossil fuels, agriculture and land use changes like deforestation. These causes emission of carbon dioxide (CO_2), the main gas responsible for climate change, as well as of other greenhouse gases.

Climate change may be due to internal processes or external forces. Some external irrelevances, such as changes in solar radiation and volcanism occur naturally and contribute to the total natural variability of the climate system. Other external changes, such as changes in the composition of the atmosphere that began with industrial revolution, are the result of human activity.[2] Greenhouse gases form a natural blanket in the atmosphere which keeps the planet warm enough for lite i.e. at 15°C. Greenhouse Gases are carbon dioxide (CO_2), hydroflurocarbons (HFC's), Per fluorocarbons (OFCs), Sulphur hexafluoride (SF_6). Human caused emissions of greenhouse gases have made the blanket thicker, trapping heat and leading to *global warming*. Fossil fuels are the single biggest source of human generated greenhouse gas emissions.

Incidentally it is coal, a fossil fuel that is burnt in maximum of Power Generation Plants across the world. Liquid fuels of course have their own share of guilt.

When energy from the sun enters the Earth's atmosphere, about a third of it is reflected back to space. Of the rest, the atmosphere absorbs some, bet most of it is absorbed by the surfaces of the earth. The Earth emits energy at the longer wavelength. Some of this energy escapes to space but some is absorbed again and remitted by clouds and the greenhouse gases such as carbon dioxide, methane and nitrous oxide. This helps to warm the surface and the troposphere, keeping warmer than it would otherwise be. This is Global warming.

Threat to Earth

- **Increased Warming** - The average global temperature went up by about 0.74°C during the 20th century with the warming affecting land more than ocean areas.
- **More CO_2** - Carbon dioxide is the dominate contributor to current climate change.
- **More water but not every where** - More precipitation has been observed in the northern region as compared to southern parts of the planet. More intense and longer draughts have been observed over wide areas since 1970's.
- **Glacier melting** – Gangotri Glacier is retreating at a special of about 30 meters a year threatening the existence of perennial river Ganga. If warming continues then Glaciers all over the world will nelt rapidly, causing dry periods with very little water flowing in the river.
- **Rise in sea level** – Due to melting of Glaciers, the average rise in sea level has been 0.17 meters in 20th century as compared to 19th century. The average temperature of the global ocean has also increased. It is amazing that one meter rise in sea level would displace of million people.
- **Arctic warming** – Average Arctic temperature has increased at almost twice the global average rate in the past 100 years. Satellite data shows that the averageArctic Sea ice extent has shrunk by 2.7 percent per decade.
- **Marine ecosystem** i.e. flora and fauna are adversely affected due to rise in temperature of global waters.

- **Heat waves –** The most obvious impact of global warming which will be the direct effect on planet will experience more extreme heat waves.
- **Extreme events and Disasters** - Melting glaciers and disturbed rainfall patterns will trigger off floods, landslides, debris flows and droughts.
- **Infections Diseases** – According to World Health Organization (WHO) climate change will have serious and damaging impact on human health in South East Asia including India. The six diseases that would adversely impact human health are respiratory diseases, vector borne diseases (Malaria and dengue), water-born diseases (diarrhea and cholera), malnutrition, injuries and psychological stress.

International Negotiations : Initiative by UN

On climate change and Global Warming, public concern about the worlds climate mounted in 1980's and as a result WMO (World Meteorological Organisation) and the UNEP (United Nations Environmental Programme) established the IPCC (Intergovernmental panel on climate change) in 1988 to assess the seriousness of the problem. The first Assessment report of IPCC came in 1990 which highlighted the global threat of climate change.

In December 1990, the UN General Assembly decided to launch negotiation on what was to become UNFCC (United Nations Framework Convention on climate change) signed in *Earth summit,* held in *Rio de Janeiro in 1992.* This treaty is aimed at stabilizing greenhouse gas concentrations in the atmosphere at a level that would prevent dangerous effects of climate change. It came into force in 1994 after being ratified by 50 countries.

In 1997, the parties to UNFCC adopted the *Kyoto Protocol,* which required Annex 1 countries (developed countries) to reduce their overall GHG emission by 5.2% below their 1990 levels. The goal is to lower overall emissions of six greenhouse gases. Kyoto Protocol treaty was negotiated in Kyoto, Japan in December 1997, opened for signature in March 1998 and closed in 1999. *The agreements come into force on February 2005. By early 2008, 177 countries had officially committed (ratified) to the Protocol but still not including USA and a handful of small countries.*

Most of the industrialized nations and some central European economies in transition (Annex B countries) agreed to legally binding reductions in greenhouse gas emissions to an average of 6 to 8% below 1990 levels between the year 2008-2012 (first emission budget period). United States is required to reduce its total emission to an average of 7 percent below 1990 levels. For three countries namely New Zealand, Russia and Ukraine, the target was set at parity with 1990 emission levels and for other three i.e. Australia, Iceland, Norway targets were actually allowed to be above 1990 emissions level due to special circumstances in those countries.

A key feature Kyoto protocol was that, aside from Japan, no specific reduction targets were set for any country in Asia, Africa or Latin America. All developing countries committed themselves to broad policy goals for controlling their greenhouse gas emissions and the 'Kyoto mechanisms' were set up to encourage developed countries adopt low-emission technologies and to provide for 'emission trading' between countries.

Overall greenhouse gas emission for the 40 developed nations declined by almost 5% from 1990 to 2005. A few Western European countries have been relatively successful in meeting their targets. Of the major sources of emission, France, UK and Germany achieved reduction of 7, 15 and 19 percent respectively. In contrast, emissions increased by more then 50% in Canada, Spain and Turkey. *Emission from the USA increased by 16 percent. While this is far from the worst performance among the developed countries, it matters a lot as USA contributes to about a third of all global emissions.*

Bringing the protocol into force, it repaired rectification by at least 55 countries. *Meeting this requirement was far from automatic, and the treaty's prospects seemed dim when President Bush announced in 2001 that the USA, while accepting in principle, the need to control greenhouse gas emissions, would not ratify the Protocol as long as it imposed binding targets on some countries while excusing others, notably China and India.* The Protocol was adjusted at a meeting in Bonn in 2001 in an attempt to persuade relevant countries to commit it. As a result Russia and Japan in 2004 complied with the treaty. And this satisfied the 55% requirement bringing the Protocol into force in Feb. 2005. By 2008, 177 countries have signed but still not including the USA and handful of small countries. It is surprising that U.S. the world leader, resort to bargaining tactics.

Mechanisms

The Kyoto Protocol provides for three mechanisms that enable developed countries with quantified emission limitation and reduction commitments to acquire greenhouse gas reduction credits. These mechanisms are Joint Implementation (JI), Clean Development Mechanism (CDM) and International Emission Trading (IET). Under JI, a developed country with relatively high costs of domestic greenhouse reduction would set up a project in another developed country, that has a relatively low cost. Under CDM, a developed country can take up a greenhouse gas reduction project activity in a developing country where the cost of greenhouse gas reduction project activities is usually much lower. The developed country would be given credits for meeting its emission reduction targets, while the developing country would receive the capital and clean technology to implement the project. Under IET, countries can trade in the international carbon credit market. Countries with surplus credits can sell them to countries with quantified emission limitation and reduction commitments under the Kyoto Protocol.

Carbon Trading – A Clever Bargain of the West

Carbon credits create a market for reducing greenhouse emissions by giving a monetary value to the cost of polluting the air. This means that carbon becomes a cost of business and is seen like other inputs such as raw materials or labor. By way of example, assume a factory produces 100,000 tonnes of greenhouse emissions in a year. The government then enacts a law that limits the maximum emissions a business can have. So the factory is given a quota of say 80,000 tonnes or is required to purchase carbon credits to offset the excess. A business would buy the carbon credits on an open market from organizations that have been approved as being able to sell legitimate carbon credits. One seller might be a company that will plant so many trees for every carbon credit you buy from them. So, for this factory, it might pollute a ton, but is essentially now paying another group to go out and plant trees which will, say, draw a ton of carbon dioxide from the atmosphere, As emission levels are predicted to keep rising over time, it is envisioned that the number of companies wanting/needing to buy more credits will increase, which will push the market price up and encourage more groups to undertake environmental friendly activities that create for them carbon credits to sell.

Carbon credits are a tradable permit scheme. They provide a way to reduce greenhouse gas emissions by giving them a monetary value. A credit gives the owner the right to emit one ton of carbon dioxide. Carbon credits are provided as certificates, awarded to countries that are successful in reducing emissions of greenhouse gases. The concept of carbon credits came into existence as a result of increasing awareness of the need for pollution control. It was formalized in the Kyoto Protocol, an international agreement between 169 countries.

Carbon Trading is market based mechanisms in which carbon trading markets are developed that bring buyers and sellers of carbon credits together with standardized rules of trade. Kyoto Protocol set quotas on the amount of greenhouse gases that countries can produce. Countries, in turn, set quotas on the emissions by businesses. Businesses that are over their quotas must buy carbon credits for their excess emissions, while businesses that are below their quotas can sell their remaining credits. By allowing credits to be bought and sold, a business for which reducing its emissions would be expensive or prohibitive, can pay another business to make the reduction for it. This minimizes the quota's impact on the business, while still reaching the quota for trading emissions. Such a credit can be sold in the international market at the prevailing market price. *As a matter of fact, Carbon Credit policy is hardly a deterrent for the excessive emissions can always be offset by monetary transactions. On the other hand, it is an allurement for third world Countries to compromise with their developmental needs by selling credits for money involving self deception and self denial. On the contrary, the Developed Nations can go on with more emissions by throwing dollars to make up for their irresponsibility.*

The Heat of Politics

Let us see the reactions of the world nations to Kyoto Protocol and the issues. The first leader of U.S putting Global Warming on the political agenda was *Richard Nixon* in 1969 during his presidential tenure. Nixon wanted environmental topics (as acid rain and greenhouse effect) to be treated by a third and civil pillar of NATO. The reaction of the NATO allies was lukewarm but the initiative gained impact in the civil field. In the 1980s, *Margaret Thatcher* the then Prime Minister of England was instrumental in increasing the United Kingdom's electricity generation from North Sea gas and reducing generation from coal.[3] This was an exemplary step by England so early as in 80s. Most of the Western countries have ratified the Kyoto Protocol. But in U.S Democratic Congress refuses to take a vote on it and thus the United States is not bound to the treaty.

The U.S president *Barack Obama* supports passage of the *American Clean Energy and Security Act* to establish a *United States Carbon Cap and Trade Program.* "We are not going to ratify the Kyoto Protocol. That is out," said US climate negotiator Jonathan Pershing at the 2009 Bangkok Climate Change Talks[4] . It is a smart move by U.S shedding its global responsibility.

The international climate conference in Copenhagen ended with a *watered-down agreement* that some observers believe will be ineffective in slowing global warming.[5] The three-page accord that Mr. Obama negotiated with the leaders of China, India, Brazil and South Africa and then presented to the Conference did not meet even the modest expectations that leaders set for this meeting, notably by failing to set a 2010 goal for reaching a binding international treaty to seal the provisions of the accord. The plan does not either firmly commit the industrialized nations or the developing nations to firm targets for midterm or long-term reductions of greenhouse gas emissions. Nonetheless the accord is significant in that it codifies the commitments of individual nations to act on their own to tackle *global warming*.

The accord also provides a system for monitoring and reporting progress towards those national pollution-reduction goals, a compromise on an issue over which China bargained hard. It calls for hundreds of billions of dollars to flow from wealthy nations to those countries most vulnerable to a changing climate. The laudable consensus is that the Accord sets a goal of limiting the global temperature rise to 2 degrees celsius above preindustrial levels by 2050; it implies deep cuts in climate-altering emissions over the next forty years. But it was not an unequivocal agreement to many because it was not an encouraging outcome to a two-year process that had the goal of producing a comprehensive and enforceable action plan for addressing dangerous changes to the global climate. The clumsy compromise mirrored the chaotic nature of the conference, which virtually all participants said had been badly organized and conducted.

Sudanese diplomat- Lumumba Stanislaus Di-Aping, representing the Group of 77 developing countries, denounced the accord saying that "The *developed* countries have decided that damage to *developing* countries is acceptable," ....that the 2-degree target would result in massive devastation to Africa and small island states." He and many other representatives of the most vulnerable countries wanted a target of 1.5 degrees. The comments of Sudan reflect the helplessness of the Developing Countries. The highhanded attitude of many of the developed countries especially that of U.S smacks of capitalist domination. Holding the developing countries responsible for not being responsibly handling global warming is escapism the West is well versed in.

Need for Positive Action from the Advanced Countries

The *global warming* is not only a scientific phenomenon but it also has acquired strong political overtones in the last few decades in the world. The advanced countries in Europe and the United States of America though are the main culprits for increasing emission of CO_2 in their countries, it is surprising that they have great expectations from the developing countries i.e. Asia, Africa, Latin America and South-East Asia, with regard to positive actions for controlling global warming. The amount of sincerity required to be shown in the efforts to collectively control the global warming syndrome, the advanced countries have not been sincere. The neo-colonialist and neo-imperialistic tendencies of the super-powers such as USA, France, England cannot escape the critical eye. These nations have virtually indulged in economic imperialism in the entire world by way of global control of markets through multinational companies. Besides capturing the third world markets such as India, South-East Asia, Pakistan etc., where the production technologies have not caught up with the modern trend as yet, an orchestrated campaign is unleashed by the developed countries to discourage the developing countries in terms of industrialization and economic growth. In the name of global warming, the advanced countries are bullying and brow-beating the developing the countries. The question arises is whether, it is only the developing countries who are supposed to control the global warming or is it the super power US, which needs to be more transparent in its appeal to the world and translate it's promises into action. It is a known fact that the developing countries suffer from poverty, unemployment, mal-nutrition, disease and are putting their best foot forward to catch up with the rest of the world in terms of quality of life and security for their citizens. Truly speaking, it is the responsibility of the advanced countries to seriously resolve to control the excessive emissions of harmful gases causing the global warming. Or else the blame game the Western countries are indulged in, would only lead to half-hearted efforts in controlling climate change and eventually prove detrimental to the entire mankind. Carbon Trading is nothing but shifting the responsibility of reducing of emissions on the developing countries.

The Western world, historically, has been infamous for causing political un-stability in Asia and Africa. The first world war and the second world war have been marked by excessive ambition for power and subjugation of weaker nations. The post-world war scenario was nothing but a story of cold war between the USA and the Soviet Union until 1992. After the disintegration of Soviet Union in 1992, the United States has virtually emerged as the un-crowned king and emperor of the world making its presence felt in every nook and corner. China being the largest communist country in the world has been pre-occupied in its programmes of development and has not taken sufficient initiative towards balance of power in the world. The northern and southern hemisphere of the globe is clearly polarized by developed and developing nations and it is no longer a secret that the latter always have to satisfy themselves with a raw deal in many areas of development. It is high time, the North has realized that its existence is not independent of the South. The progress, the prosperity and wealth of the northern countries is correlated to the existence and growth of the countries of the Southern Hemisphere. Therefore, it is important for the western world to realize this truth and make sincere, concerted and meaningful efforts to arrest the global warming as *"charity begins at home"*. It is these countries who are supposed to take lead and exemplify to the rest of the world. However it is not to waive the individual liabilities of the Developing Countries any way. The essence is that there is need for united action with sincere partnership among all nations to fight the impending danger of climate change.

Equality between Unequals ?

The expectations of Developed Nations from the Developing Nations are anything but reasonable. The latter stand on a totally different footing with regard to development needs and priorities. Poor infrastructure, low industrial growth indicators, massive unemployment, malnutrition, disease are some of the serious issues the developing countries are faced with that need to be addressed with quick developmental strategies. Energy is sine-qua-non for these countries even if it involves emissions beyond accepted limits. Restricting the developing countries on par with the developed ones is unjustified. In the name reduction of emissions, these countries may suffer from underdevelopment for eternity while the Developed are already saturated with high levels of indicators of development and human life. There can be an agreement on equal terms between Unequals. Majority of Developing countries do not have provision of electricity for rural house holds and let alone industries. Many countries do not have even industries for manufacturing of defense equipments or even Consumer goods. They are, today, far from being in a position to cause global warming of their share and threaten the climate or the mother Earth. The mechanism of reducing emissions must have an element of protection towards poor and struggling nations.

A Different Note

The Canadian climatologist Timothy Ball says that the widely propagated "fact" that humans are contributing to global warming, is the "greatest deception in the history of science." Ball has made no friends among global warming alarmists by saying that global warming is caused by the sun, that global warming will be good for human life and that the Kyoto Protocol "is a political solution to a nonexistent problem without scientific justification." Needless to say, Ball strongly disagrees with the findings of the latest report from the United Nations' Intergovernmental Panel on Climate Change, which on Feb. 2 concluded that it is "very likely" that global warming is the result of human activity. Denouncing the IPCC report he feels that it's also the political agenda of a group of people ... who believe that industrialization and development and capitalism and the Western way is a terrible system and they want to bring it down.[6] They couldn't do it by attacking energy because they know that would get the public's back up very quickly. ... The vehicle they chose was CO2, because that's the byproduct of industry and fossil-fuel burning, which ofcourse drives the whole thing. It appears that Timothy Ball is the voice of some of the Western Nations atleast. Nevertheless he can be quoted on any light hearted occasion.

REFERENCES

1. United Nations framework convention (UNFCC) on climate change.
2. Fourth Assessment Report, Intergovernmental Panel on climate change (IPCC)
3. (Murray, Iain (2003-09-17). (*"Fixing the Game:Kyoto rules"*. National Review Online. *http://www.nationalreview.com/comment/comment-murray091703.asp*. Retrieved 2010-01-20.)
4. Hood, Marlowe (2009-10-08). *"Climate: What's to become of the Kyoto Protocol?"*. AFP. *http://www.google.com/hostednews/afp/article/ALeqM5jSFWRYM8O_rQkQwLMBNKCsF0A2ag. Retrieved 2009-10-10.*)
5. *http://livingstories.googlelabs.com/lsps/climatechange#OVERVIEW:false,false,fal*se,n,n,n:141007;sp:0;
6. *www.pitsberglive.com.*

15
Protection of Girl Children : A National Cause

Introduction

Women liberation is the hall mark of modern civilization. Almost all the nations in the world have recognized the need for empowerment of women in order to emancipate them from the clutches of age old oppression perpetrated by the society against them in one form or the other. Western countries are way ahead in this mission in comparison to the third world. India has awakened and of course risen to the occasion in time, with the dawn of independence. The Constitution has made provisions for the development of women and children in chapter III and IV by way of Fundamental Rights and Directive Principles of State policy. Chapter III of the Constitution through article 15(3) makes special provisions for women and children.

The most revolutionary development happened in India is the enactment of the Hindu Succession Act 1956 and the Hindu Marriage Act 1955. These two acts have recognized the status of a women for the first time in India as equal to that of men. For the first ever time, a provision for divorce was made in law and, equally the consent of a women for a marriage, besides the qualifying age for marriage, were made compulsory. The Hindu Succession Act 1956 recognizes the right to property to a woman as opposed to the ancient schools of thought - the Mitakshara and Dayabhaga. The Indian Succession Act of 1925 was equally a progressive legislation recognizing the importance of women in matters of property. Over the years, the law in India has been so improved to provide equal status to women in all fields. Many states in the country have already made provisions for reservation for women in Govt. Services. In short, the conditions required for an equal development of women in India do exist at least in law. However female feticide and neglect of girl children are common in the country in spite of legislations and schemes for development of women. The question is, what is it that is enslaving a woman in India still and where do we start from in addressing the issue?

It is unfortunate that, India, whose citizens worship women goddesses has a peculiar society crippled with a mindset of a discouraging women. The malady is so much so that, even a large percentage of women prefer male children to female ones. It is common story that in many parts of the country, voluntary or forced abortions take place to get rid of a female fetus. Despite there being a law against such offence, the practice is on with the connivance of professionals, doctors and the parents. It is not surprising that the average indicators of health, protection, education and empowerment of women in India are far from satisfactory. Neglect of girl child is serious problem in India which failed to receive required amount of attention. The recent census of 2010 also reflects a discouraging picture of women of sex ratio in many States.

Neglected and Exploited

The following facts and figures depict the miserable situation of girl children in the country:-

1. To begin with, the sex ratio as per 2001 census is 927 girls per 1000 boys for the population aged between 0-6 years. The NFHS –III in its own survey after a gap of 5 years since census, found out that this has further fallen down to 918 in the entire country. It

was also found that in rural areas, the ratio has come down to 921 lower than what the census reported (934). This shows that there is a decline in the birth rate of girl children in the country which is not a sign of positive orientation towards girl children[1].

2. Though neo-natal mortality rate is better among the girls as the children grow the rate is higher in comparison to boys. It is 36% higher than males during the post neo-natal period and 61% higher than males between 1-4 years of infant stage[2].

3. Girl children in India as per the study reports are exposed to rape, trafficking, sexual abuse and exploitation, beggary and child labour. The study on child abuse conducted by Ministry of WCD Department in the year 2007 came up with a fact that two-thirds of girls were neglected and around 50% girls wished that they were boys. Similarly, around 70% girls were assigned house-hold work whereas around 50% of the girls were entrusted the job of looking after their siblings. The report says that this is a great deprivation of opportunities for girl children[3].

4. Child marriages it seems no longer remained a thing of the past. As per the NFHS – II, some states in the country still report around 60% of incidents especially in rural areas. The details are as under :

   Jharkhand 71%, Rajasthan 61.7%, Bihar, 65.2%, West Bengal 62.6%, Madhya Pradesh 62%, Andhra Pradesh 61.4. Uttar Pradesh 61.1%, Chhattisgarh 60.3%[4].

5. The child bearing between 15-19 years of girls is reported to be around 15% among women as per NFHS-III survey. It is also reported that it is 19% in rural areas whereas in urban areas it is just 9%. Jharkhand, West Bengal and Bihar are with more than 25% of women between 15-19 years bearing children[5].

The above facts are glaring revelations of the miserable state of young and adolescent girls in the country that need sound policy intervention and pragmatic initiative. It is unfortunate that in a developing country like India, the condition of girl children and young girls besides adult women is so pathetic that even after 60 years of independence, the issue of women empowerment and women liberation have not been addressed earnestly to bring about required changes.

It is surprising that despite constitutional guarantees of justice, social, economic and political and assurances of a life of freedom, equality and dignity, sexual abuse and other heinous crime are ravaging the lives of millions of women who remain a prey to predator in the form of husbands, relatives or friends. The life of an average Indian women is still governed by customs, habits, prejudices and unwritten codes of conduct. It is normally seen that the incidence of rape, dowry death, torture, molestation and eve-teasing have been on the rise despite the omni-presence of law and law enforcing machinery. A casual look at the media coverage in no way gives relief from the past. On the contrary, the picture is more demoralizing besides horrifying.

The international scenario with regard to girl children and adolescent girls is not very different from India. There are more than 100 countries where girl children are subjected to child labour, trafficking, prostitution, pornography etc. The data provided by UNICEF vouches for this fact. As per data, 12,00,000 children are becoming victims of trafficking in the entire world whereas 6,00,000 children are subjected to illicit activities. More pathetic situation is that 18,00,000 children are drawn into prostitution and pornography while 3,00,000 children have become victims of armed conflicts across the globe[6]. Many women before they could attain 18 years were married off against their consent in developing countries. The syndrome is more appalling in rural areas than in urban[7].

In sub-Saharan Africa, it is 48% whereas in the rest and Central Africa, it is 56%. In South-East Asia, it is 54% and even in Latin American and Carribbean countries, it is 31%. In all the developing countries, excluding China 45% children are married off before 18 years while the percentage is 57% in the least developed countries[8] The United Nations has prescribed Millennium Development Goals for all the member nations to follow and achieve by 2015 in which the rights of children and especially those of girl children and adolescent girls have been emphasized.

The MGD have the following priorities for the protection of children in the world:-

The links between child protection and the Millennium Development Goals

S.No.	*Millennium Development Goal*	*Child Protection Consideration*
1.	Eradicate extreme poverty and hunger	• Child labour squanders a nation's human capital. • Poverty and exclusion contributes to child abandonment and to the overuse of formal and informal fostering arrangements or institutional care, leading to poor child development. • Legal systems that do not take into account the child's age and fail to promote reintegration into the community of children in conflict with the law increase the likelihood of their poverty and marginalization.
2.	Achieve universal primary education	• Child labour prevents children from attending school.

		• Child marriage leads to the removal of girls form school. • Children without parental care must be placed in an appropriate family environment to increase the likelihood they will receive an education.
3.	Promote gender equality and empower women	• Girls are disproportionately engaged in domestic work, which compromises their school participation. • Child marriage leads to the removal of girls form school and may limit their opportunities to participate in the public life of their communities. • Violence and harassment in schools are obstacles to gender equality in education. Sexual violence, exploitation and abuse undermine efforts to empower women and girls.
4.	Reduce child mortality	• Violence against children can lead to child mortality. • Child marriage and early childbearing lead to higher risks of maternal mortality and morbidity.
5.	Improve maternal health	• Child marriage jeopardizes both maternal and infant health. • Female Genital Mutilation/ Cutting increases the chance of maternal mortality during delivery and complications thereafter.

6.	Combat HIV/AIDS, malaria and other diseases	• Sexual exploitation, abuse and violence can lead to the infection of girls and boys. • Children in HIV/AIDS-affected families are particularly at risk of losing the care and protection of their families.

Source: (Information supplied by Child Protection Section, Programme Division, UNICEF, New York, 2006).

The above table of the primary goals of Millennium development and consideration of protection of children including girls throws light on the responsibilities and duties of the Government and society. Though child protection is a concern the protection of girl child becomes a topmost priority in view of the vulnerable state of existence of girls. The Millennium Development Goals have a time frame to be accomplished and achieved. 2015 AD is the deadline stipulated by United Nation to fulfill these goals by all member nations.

What is the Constitutional Position?

In the light of these, miserable state of women and children (includes Girl Children) in India, the Protection guaranteed the article 23 and article 15(4), turns out to be a farce. What these Articles envisage is as below :

Article 23 (1) : Traffic in human beings and beggar and other similar forms of forced labour are prohibited and any contravention of this provision shall be an offence punishable in accordance with law.

(2) Nothing in this article shall prevent the State from imposing compulsory service for public purposes, and in imposing such service the State shall not make any discrimination on grounds only of religion, race, caste or class or any of them.

Article 15 (3) : Nothing in this article shall prevent the state from making any special provisions for women and children.

This provision as an exception to article 15(1) and (2) which prohibits discrimination on the grounds of religion, race, caste, sex and place of birth[9]. This in other words means that for protection of children positive discrimination can be made. The provisions are for protection and advancement of children. Such special provision, the hon'ble Supreme Court said, may be in the form of reservation.[10] When special reservations to be made in this regard the Court observed that there can be no limit as to the extent of the reservation with regard to 15(4) or 16(4)[11] Art.15 (3) must be read harmoniously with Art.16 to achieve the purpose for which these Articles have been framed.[12] Such special provision, it was also observed, may be made either by legislation or by executive order.[13] The constitutional provisions are no doubt, exemplary in so far as protection to the children to be accorded by the state is concerned. However, the question remains to be addressed is as to the efficacy of legislations made in tune with these provisions.

It is an irony that despite the enactment of acts such as Child Labour Prohibition Act 1986 and as amended in 2006, and Prohibition of immoral Trafficking Act, the uncontrolled exploitation of young children continues. It is again an area of debate as to the real reason for the failures of the statutes in this context. The enforcement agencies (the state machinery such as Police, Judiciary, Protection Homes) are somewhere lacking in the capacity or in determination in effectively rising to the occasion. Besides it is also possible that the laws made in this regard and the punishments prescribed are suffering from some lacunae due to which the culprits manage to go scot-free.

The National Human Rights Commission in its Annual Report 1999-2000 comes out with effective recommendations with regard to the protection of children and their rights where in it specifically emphasises protection of Girl Children when it recommends on page 165, annexure II.

"That the State ensure that legislation criminalizes the sexual exploitation of children and penalizes all the offenders involved, whether local or foreign, while ensuring that the child victims of this practice are not penalized. While noting that Devadasi, or ritual prostitution, is prohibited under the law, the Commission recommends that the State takes all necessary steps to eradicate this practice."

Some of the Important Legislations

The recommendations of the National Human Rights Commission with regard to rights of children in India have to a great extent been translated into action by quite a few legislations in the country. Some of the important recommendations were translated in to action by legislations as under.

1. Child Labour (Prohibition and Regulation) Act,1986
2. Prohibition of Child Marriage Act 2006
3. Juvenile Justice (Care and Protection of Children) Act, 2000
4. Factories Act, 1954
5. Probation of Offenders Act, 1958
6. Bonded Labour System (Abolition) Act, 1976
7. Bombay Prevention of Begging Act, 1959
8. Immoral Traffic Prevention Act, 1986
9. Commission for Protection of the Rights of the Child Act, 2005

New Initiatives by the Government

The Government of India through the Ministry of Women and Child Development has taken special initiatives with regard to the protection and development of Girl Children and Adolescent Girls. This is a new area, unheard till now, is extremely becoming important in view of the emphasis given on the subject by NCRC (National Child

Rights Commission). The policy of the government of India in relation to Girl Children and Adolescent Girls is based on the following priorities :

(a) Creating and enabling environment,

(b) Increasing choices and,

(c) Promoting development through special opportunities.

In accordance with these priorities, the government has devised NPAC 2005 known as National Plan of Action for Children with an objective to include goals, objectives, strategies with the time plan to empower the girl child. The Ministry of Women and Child Development committed to bring attitudinal changes and eradicate discriminatory practices towards girls. In this respect, the campaign was initiated through social political and religious leaders and with the help of all the government departments, serious concern was given to enforce or amend the laws in order to protect the rights of the girl child and ensure equality between girl and boy. Besides, gender sensitization was undertaken as a programme for all public authorities including judiciary and police. NGOs and CBOs were promoted by the government to seek their voluntary contribution in the mission. It is very heartening to know that the 11th five-year plan has pro-active affirmative approaches and necessary actions for protecting the rights of the girl child. The onus is also given to Panchayats, Gramsabhas, CBOs and district authorities to monitor the overall progress.

Legislative Interventions

The Government though enacted the pre-conception and pre-natal diagnostic technique [prohibition of sex selection (PCPNDT Act 1994)]. The prosecution of offenders needs to be exemplary. The data available from states and union territories shows that 34,012 institutions using ultrasound, image-scanners etc. have been registered under this act whereas, in the year 2008, there were 420 cases pending in the courts and police stations for violating the law. It is surely an achievement that 165 ultrasound machines were seized and sealed during the prosecution. The state governments were regularly directed in this regard to take effective steps in disposing of pending cases. There have been some convictions in this connection in Punjab, Haryana and Rajasthan. In response to a direction by the court, the government of India has constituted the National Inspection and Monitoring Committee to investigate the ground realities in matters connected with PCPNDT Act 1994[14].

In order to fight the trafficking and abduction syndrome of girl children, the Ministry of Women and Child Development had come up with a national plan of action in 1998 primarily to eradicate trafficking for commercial sexual exploitation of girl children and women. The Ministry of Women and Child Development, in collaboration with the Ministry of Home Affairs, National Human Rights Commission and the National Commission for Women (NCW) is in the process of developing an Integrated Plan of Action to Prevent and Combat Human Trafficking, with Special Focus on Children and Women, to make it more comprehensive, so as to cover 'trafficking in persons' for any purpose.[15]

With regard to protection of children from sexual and physical abuse, special emphasis was provided by the NPAC 2005. National Commission for Protection of Child Rights was formed to address exploitation of children. Adoption of the Juvenile Justice (JJ) Act 2007 along with the rules is a very important development in this first decade of 21st century.

Developmental Initiatives

The government in addition to legislations made in matters of protection of girl children has also initiated developmental programmes through Integrated Child Development Scheme from mid 1980s. The scheme intended to protect children of age group 0-6 years by caring for their health, nutrition and pre-school education. Supplementary Nutrition Programme has been a great success in the country ever since. Today, we see in each village an Anganwadi functioning attending to children of the age-group below 6 years in matters of health, hygiene and pre-school training. Incidentally, the participation of young children in Anganwadi Centres is very encouraging. Besides young children programmes for the empowerment and development of adolescent girls has also been the priority of the government. Adolescent has been defined by WHO as the period of life spanning between 10-19 years and the youth as between 15-24 years. The government has also initiated programmes for the development and empowerment of these adolescent girls.

Some of these are as under :

(a) Kishor Shakti Yojana – for improving the health and nutritional status of girls.

(b) Balika Samridhi Yojana – To delay the age of marriage.

(c) Nehru Yuva Kendras – for awareness generation through active participation of youth.

(d) Mahila Samaikhya Programme – providing equal access to education facilities for adolescent girls and young women.

(e) School AIDS education.

(f) University talks AIDS.

(g) Training of Rural Youth for Self Employment (TRYSEM).

(h) Reproductive and Child Health Programme.

Apart from the above routine schemes meant for women and girls, the government of India has introduced two important and revolutionary schemes for the benefit of girl children which are as under :

Dhanlaxmi Yojna

In accordance with chapter IV article 17 of Commission for Protection of Child Right Act 2005, in order to check female foeticide and promote girls' education, Dhanlaxmi Yojna has been started by GOI. This scheme has been started in 11 blocks of India. Under this scheme family of the girl (preferably mother) is given conditional cash assistance. This *is conditional cash transfer scheme* whose terms are as under :

1. Cash assistance for birth and registration of girl.
2. For complete immunization amount is transferred at different stages.
3. For school admission and scholarship for education upto class 8th.
4. Insurance scheme in case marriage in not solemnized upto 18 years.
5. LIC will provide insurance cover of lumpsum of Rs. 01.00 Lakh plus to the girl child born on or after 19th November 2008 which will be available to the said girl child on completion of 18 years and remaining unmarried.

This scheme is in fact a direct intervention to encourage birth of girls.

SABLA

SABLA (Rajiv Gandhi Scheme for Empowerment of Adolescent Girls) is a scheme aimed at directly helping the young girls of age group 11-18 with a view to empower them in terms of personality and skill development so that they can enable themselves to stand-up on their feet when they attain the adulthood. Adolescence is a significant phase of transition from childhood to adulthood, which is marked by physical changes accompanied by psychological ones. This is the time to make adolescent girls aware of and informed about various facets of life in order to promote a healthy way of living.

Objectives of the Scheme

The objectives of the scheme are to:

(i) Enable self-development and empowerment of AGs;

(ii) Improve their nutrition and health status;

(iii) Spread awareness among them about health, hygiene, nutrition, Adolescent Reproductive and Sexual Health (ARSH), and family and child care;

(iv) Upgrade their home-based skills, life skills and vocational skills;

(v) Mainstream out-of-school AGs into formal/non formal-education; and

(vi) Inform and guide them about existing public services, such as PHC, CHC, Post Office, Bank, Police Station, etc.

Target Group

AGs of age group 11-18 years. This scheme has been launched in all ICDS projects in selected 200 districts across India on pilot basis.

Services under the scheme: There are two major components under the scheme

(i) Nutrition Component:

11-14 years AGs : Out of school girls

14-18 years AGs : All girls

(ii) Non Nutrition Component

For out of school AGs :

(a) 11-18 Years

- Nutrition provision,

- IFA supplementation,
- Health check-up and Referral services,
- Nutrition and Health Education (NHE),
- Counseling/Guidance on family welfare, ARSH, child care practices,
- Life Skill Education and accessing public services

(*b*) 16-18 Years

- Vocational training under National Skill Development Programme (NSDP)

For school going AGs of 11-18 years the services at (ii) (a) will be provided twice a month in school day and four times a month in vacations.

This scheme is introduced for the first time by government of India in 2010 with a view to address the real problems of adolescent girls in the country.

Conclusion

The schemes and programmes will have a limited impact in the absence of a radical resolution on the part of the Govt. to protect girl child and empower adolescent girls. What is essentially relevant is an all out war against factors responsible for the denial of basic rights of girls. A concerted action against inimical mind set of the society and negative social practices in very important. While addressing the issue we must bear in mind that neglect and subjugation of girls and girl Children is only a symptom of social backwardness. The disease is else where. It is the combined effect of certain maladies in our country that is responsible for backwardness. These are social inequalities, poverty, and religion. In short these are instrumental in denial of basic human rights to begin with let alone the rights of children. Let us recollect what the Supreme Court has said in Bandhua Mukti Morcha v. Union of India[16].

"This right to live with human dignity enshrined in Article 21 derives its life breath from the Directive Principles of State Policy and particularly clauses (e) and (f) of Article 39 and Article 41 and 42 and at the least therefore, it must include protection of health and strength of workers, men and women, and of the tender age of children against abuse, opportunities and facilities for children to develop in a healthy manner and in conditions of freedom and dignity, education facilities, just and humane conditions of work and maternity relief. These are the minimum requirements which must exist in order to enable a person to live with human dignity".

The honourable Supreme Court in the above paragraph was suggesting a golden mean between the fundamental rights and directive principles of state policy. It laid special emphasis on women and children of tender age which includes girls and directed that freedom, dignity are to be guaranteed to them. Here, the essence is positive action towards protection of human rights and consequently the rights of the children. We learn from this judgement that the provisions of directive principles of state policy must be implemented in order to guarantee the fundamental right of life and liberty enshrined in article 21. This calls for a strong initiative addressing the basic issues such as poverty, inequality and exploitation. In the light of the thrust given by the Supreme Court, the government has made many legislations keeping in view the essential requirements of children in their initial stage of growth. However, some important areas of concern still need more attention. Let us enumerate them as under:

Suggestions

(a) Empowerment of women is sine-qua-non for protection of girl children. A socially and economically empowered woman can enable herself to protect her children better than a man can do as *mother* happens to be natural guardian. There is a great need for economic emancipation of women in the country. Empowerment of women has different facets such as educational, social and personal.

(b) Gender budgeting is the new trend in the government which emphasizes on the accountability of the authorities in allocations and expenditure towards women centric developmental schemes and programmes. In short, gender budgeting is a positive bias towards women and their empowerment. However, many state governments and many departments in the government of India still need to ensure accountability in this regard.

(c) Education of girls has to be in a special and protective environment warding off unwanted and negative interference of parents and traditional customs. Adequate number of schools for girls are required to be sanctioned and buildings constructed so as to accommodate the existing strength and encourage new intake across the country. Education for girls is empowerment in itself.

(d) Social factors such as caste, religion are to be taken into consideration in designing schemes and programmes. Girls from scheduled castes, tribes and backward sections of the society have to be given priority in education and empowerment because girls from these sections suffer from peculiar exploitation that inhibits growth of personality.

(e) Poverty being the major factor for majority of problems faced by a common man including exploitation of women and girl children regular and permanent income generating activities must be created so that the parents/adults do not have to push their children into un-ethical or hazardous occupations for the sake of making a living. This should get the top priority in all schemes of the government so that the root cause for miseries i.e. the poverty can be eradicated.

(f) The perceptions and the mindset of the society is of course an impediment that hampers the freedom of girls. Changing the age-old value systems is a difficult task to be performed overnight. Civil society organizations, NGOs and celebrities can be encouraged to contribute in the battle against traditional mindset of the society that is adversely operating in retarding the development of girl children. Print and electronic media too can play a progressive role and the same needs to be encouraged by the government.

(g) Besides education, girls need extra-curricular activities such as sports, music, fine-arts, adventurous expeditions etc. to satisfy their urge to grow and develop into adults. These activities will be greatly responsible for liberating girls and making them modern citizens of the country free from parochial sentiments of caste, creed or language.

The above are some of the suggestions to encourage the growth and development of girl children in India. These suggestions have to be translated into real action by the government if we are seriously interested in the protection of girl children. It is of course no denying that positive results cannot be achieved overnight. Nevertheless, it is also not to discourage our determination endeavour to fight against subjugation of girl children. Protection and empowerment of girl children will not be an impossible task in a country like ours where daughters and daughter-in-laws are considered as *lakshmi* and mother goddess is worshipped right from the days of Mohenjodaro and Harappan civilizations.

References

1. 11th Five Year Plan (2007-12), Vol. II, Social Sector, Planning Commission, GoI, 2008, p. 185.
2. National Family Health Survey-3, (Ministry of Health and Family Welfare, GoI, pp. 183, 186.
3. Study on Child Abuse: India 2007, Ministry of Women and Child Development, GoI, 2007, p. 115.

4. Statistics on Women in India, National Institute of Public Cooperation and Child Development, GoI, 2007, p. 112.
5. National Family Health Survey-3, Ministry of Health and Family Welfare, GoI, pp. 94-95.
6. Report of the UNICEF, "The state of the world's children–2006".
7. Every Child Counts : New Global Estimates on Child Labour ILO, International Programme on Elimination of Child Labour, Statistical Informational Programme on Child Labour, April 2002.)
8. Multiple indicator cluster surveys (MICS) Demographic and Health Surveys (DHS) and other national service.
9. Dattaraya Motiram More v/s State of Bombay, AIR 1953 BOM. 311).
10. Toguru Sudhakar Reddy v. Govt. of A.P. AIR 1994 SC 544 (para 3) : 1993 Supp. (4) SCC 439.
11. *Ibid.,* (para 3) : 1993 Supp. (4) SCC 439)].
12. Govt. of A.P. v. P.B.Vijaykumar, (1995) 4 SCC 544 (para 3) : 1993 Supp. (4) SCC 439).
13. Balaji M.R v. State of Mysore, AIR 1963 SC 649 : 1963 Supp. (1) SCR 439; Casebook, pp. 124-25, 130)
14. Brief on Pre-Conception and Pre-Natal Diagnostic Tec miques as on May 14, 2008, Ministry of Health and Family Welfare, GoI, May 14, 2008, p. 3.
15. Integrated Plan of Action to Prevent and Combat Human Trafficking with special focus on Children and Women, http://www.nhrc.nic.in)
16. (1997) 10 SCC 549 : AIR 1997 SC 2218.

Index

D

E

F

M

N

O